## SPRING 2017

JANUARY **1 & 2 COR**
FEBRUARY **GAL-COL**
MARCH **HEB-JAMES**
APRIL **REVELATION**

**ontrack devotions**

**OnTrack Devotions: Spring 2017**
**Published by:**
Pilgrimage Educational Resources
1362 Fords Pond Road, Clarks Summit, PA 18411
www.simplyapilgrim.com

**For subscription information:**
Pilgrimage Educational Resources
1362 Fords Pond Road, Clarks Summit, PA 18411
570.504.1463
**ontrackdevotions.com**

Printed in the United States of America

Author: Dwight E. Peterson
Executive Developer: Benjamin J. Wilhite
Editor: Kristin N. Jones
Graphic design by Higher Rock Creative Studio

ISBN-13 978-0989458344
ISBN 0989458342

10 9 8 7 6 5 4 3 2 1

Everyone is at a different place in their walk with God and in their Bible study skill. Because of that, OnTrack is designed to engage four progressive user **SKILL LEVELS**. This guide will help you identify your skill level and how to use OnTrack effectively.

## IDENTIFY YOUR PERSONAL SKILL LEVEL

Be honest about your own personal level as you begin! Starting beyond your actual level can lead to unnecessary frustration and discouragement. Some level of frustration is good when learning a skill, but too much may tempt you to give up. Pay particular attention to the approach each user should take based on their current **SKILL LEVEL.**

**Level 1:** You have spent little or no time in personal Bible study and you have limited knowledge of the Bible. **FOCUS: Key Passage, Devotional Thought.**

**Level 2:** Most of your experience with the Bible is from church and/or at home. You have been taught from the Bible, but you have not consistently studied it on your own. **FOCUS: Extra Reading, Devotional Thought, answer at least the first two Daily Questions if you can.**

**Level 3:** You have a bit of experience reading the Bible on your own. Maybe it hasn't always been consistent or you are newer at it, but you are getting comfortable with it. **FOCUS: Extra Reading, Devotional Thought, answer all four Daily Questions.**

**Level 4:** You have a lot of experience in Bible study and you consistently see solid applications. **Focus: Extra Reading, Devotional Thought, all Daily Questions, and try creating your own questions.**

Every once in awhile, review your current skill level to check whether you should bump it up. You can do this on your own, with an accountability partner, or with a spiritual mentor. Aim to grow!

## HOW TO USE ONTRACK

This tool is designed to help you grow your personal Bible study skill as a key part of developing a regular personal conversation with God. You will learn to dig into the text with good questions that lead to understanding and personal life change. To get the most out of OnTrack, follow the progression below:

**PRAY.** Ask the Holy Spirit to show you exactly what He wants you to see and understand from the Word. If you are in Christ, the Holy Spirit is in you and one of His jobs is to illuminate Scripture for you. He was the person of the Godhead directly engaged in the inspiration of the Word and He knows exactly what He meant when He wrote it.

**READ THE WORD.** Always start with reading the passage first before reading the devotional thought or any other tools you use to help understand Scripture.

What God has to say is always more important than what anyone else has to say about what God has to say.

**READ THE DEVOTIONAL THOUGHT.** The purpose of this text is to frame your thinking and to spur good questions, not to tie the passage up with a neat tidy bow.

**ANSWER THE QUESTIONS.** Some days, the author provides specific questions for you to answer that will help you dig into the text a bit. Other days, you'll see the generic Observation, Interpretation, Application, and Implementation questions. These are days designed to stretch you in the process of creating your own good questions.

**ENGAGE OTHERS.** One of the key benefits of a tool like OnTrack is that others in your world are working through the same Bible passages every day and engaging the same questions. This provides accountability for you; but more than that, it gives you an opportunity to compare notes and learn with each other. Often, you will see things they did not and vice versa. Bible study can be a team sport! It will help deepen your understanding of Scripture and your relationships.

## GET ORIENTED
The following is a quick orientation to a typical OTD day. Use the sample devotional day image on the opposite page for reference.

1. **Header Bar:** It gives you the day of the week, the date, the theme, and the key passage for the day. Read the passage in your Bible BEFORE jumping to the next step!
2. **Extra Reading:** This is the complete text for the day. The key passage from the header bar will be in there, but this covers the context of the passage. If you are ready to bite off the whole chunk of Scripture, go for it!
3. **Devotional Thought:** The daily thought is designed to frame your thinking process AFTER you read the verses and BEFORE you answer the questions. It will encourage you to chew on the verses and ponder what God is telling you through His Word. The thought models for you the method of Bible study you are learning for yourself.
4. **Questions:** Each day will have four questions that help you personally work through the process of identifying what God is saying in His Word, then connecting it to your own life. Each question builds on the one before it.

## A FINAL NOTE
Be patient and consistent. It's a process. Go at a comfortable pace. Ask God to grow your skill and to give you the discipline to keep at it. It will take time, but if you stick with it, you will be able to study God's Word for yourself.

## MATTHEW 2:13-23

### WAS FULFILLED

### SAY WHAT?
Observation: What do I see?

### SO WHAT?
Interpretation: What does it mean?

**4**

### NOW WHAT?
Application: How does it apply to me?

### THEN WHAT?
Implementation: What do I do?

Whenever a phrase is repeated in a passage, it is generally a sign that it is there for a reason. There is a significant phrase used many times in today's reading that falls into this category. Did you notice it? It is the phrase, "was fulfilled." One of the reasons the book of Matthew was written was to show the nation of Israel that Jesus Christ was the Messiah. Matthew needed to demonstrate that Jesus had a rightful claim to the throne, and that He was the fulfillment of the Old Testament prophecies. Throughout this book, the phrase "was fulfilled" is used to describe who Jesus Christ truly was. Every decision that Joseph and Mary made in today's reading is a fulfillment of prophecy about the Messiah made thousands of years before. How could the Jews have missed what is so obvious to us? As you read this book, count the number of times you read the phrase, "was fulfilled," or "to fulfill." Hopefully, as the number increases, you will have even greater confidence that Jesus Christ was the Messiah sent from God to take away our sin. May that confidence cause you to tell others who Jesus Christ is! The people in our world need know.

**3**

**XTRA READING**
MATTHEW 2

**2**

THEREFORE, IF ANYONE IS IN CHRIST, HE IS A NEW CREATION. THE OLD HAS PASSED AWAY; BEHOLD, THE NEW HAS COME.

2 CORINTHIANS 5:17 (ESV)

OnTrackDevotions.com

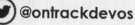 @ontrackdevos

facebook.com/ontrackdevos

# ontrack devotions

## JANUARY
### 2017
1 & 2 CORINTHIANS

# MONTHLY PRAYER SHEET

"...The prayer of a righteous man is powerful and effective." James 5:16

| Reach out... | How I will do it... | How it went... |
| --- | --- | --- |
| | | |

| Other requests... | Answered | How it was answered... |
| --- | --- | --- |
| | | |

**Name:** _____

This sheet is designed to help you make personal commitments each month that will help you grow in your walk with God. Fill it out by determining

1. What will push you
2. What you think you can achieve

If you need help filling out your commitments, seek out someone you trust who can help you. Share your commitments with those who will help keep you accountable to your personal commitment.

## Personal Devotions:
How did I do with my commitment last month? _____
I will commit to read the OnTrack Bible passage and devotional thought _____ day(s) each week this month.

## Church Attendance:
How did I do last month with my attendance? _____
I will attend Youth/Growth Group _____ time(s) this month.
I will attend the Sunday AM service _____ time(s) this month.
I will attend the Sunday PM service _____ time(s) this month.
I will attend _____ time(s) this month.
I will attend _____ time(s) this month.

## Scripture Memory:
How did I do with Scripture memory last month? _____
I will memorize _____ key verse(s) from the daily OnTrack Devotions this month.

## Outreach:
How did I do last month with sharing Christ? _____
I will share Christ with _____ person/people this month.
I will serve my local church this month by _____

## Other Activities:
List any other opportunities such as events, prayer group, etc., that you will participate in this month. _____

The book of Proverbs was designed to help us in "attaining wisdom and discipline; in understanding words of insight; in acquiring a disciplined and prudent life, doing what is right and just and fair; in giving prudence to the simple, knowledge and discretion to the young." As you read through this chapter, write down the verses that are most significant to you in your present circumstances.

VERSE | WHAT TRUTH IT COMMUNICATES | HOW IT IMPACTS MY LIFE

## 1 CORINTHIANS 1:1-9                                   MISSING?

### SAY WHAT?
Observation: What do I see?

### SO WHAT?
Interpretation: What does it mean?

### NOW WHAT?
Application: How does it apply to me?

### THEN WHAT?
Implementation: What do I do?

Have you ever compared your church with another church and wished you had what they have? Ever thought to yourself, "If only we had more kids, different leaders, a nicer facility," etc? If so, this chapter can be helpful. The Corinthian church had many problems. It would have been easy for them to conclude that their problems were related to what they did not have. Paul told them their experiences with failure were not because they were lacking anything. He told them, in verse 5, that they had been enriched in every way--in their speaking and in their knowledge. God was at work when people spoke and when people listened. In verse 7, he told them they did not lack any spiritual gift. God had given them every gift they needed to be successful as a church. The reality was their failures were not related to what they did not have. The same is true of your church. If there are struggles in your youth group or your church, it is not because of what you are missing, but because of what you or your members are not using. Maybe you are one of those parts not using what you have. How can you use what God has given you to influence your church?

**XTRA READING**
1 CORINTHIANS 1

## PRIORITIES

What is your main goal in life? What occupies your thoughts more than anything else? What do your goals and your thoughts reveal about what is really important to you? In this chapter, we learn the answers to those questions in the life of the Apostle Paul. Hopefully, they are the answers you would also give to those questions. In verse 2, Paul said his main goal was to know Christ. He had a passion and love for Christ that motivated him to pursue greater intimacy with Christ. He didn't spend time in the Scriptures to preach great messages, but to know Christ better. His goal was not to go down in history as the greatest preacher of all time; he just wanted to know Christ. Spending time with Paul would have confirmed what we already know--that his primary goal in life was to know Christ. What is your ambition in life? Is it being popular, rich, or famous? Is it being successful in sports or music? Is it your significant other? You can tell by observing how a person spends his time and what occupies his mind. Use today's questions to help you honestly examine your priorities to determine what is really most important in your life.

### SAY WHAT?
What activities occupy most of your time?

### SO WHAT?
What activities occupy your thoughts?

### NOW WHAT?
How does your pursuit of knowing Christ compare to what is listed above?

### THEN WHAT?
In light of this passage, what personal commitment can you make?

**XTRA READING**
1 CORINTHIANS 2

## 1 CORINTHIANS 3:1-9

### SAY WHAT?
Observation: What do I see?

### SO WHAT?
Interpretation: What does it mean?

### NOW WHAT?
Application: How does it apply to me?

### THEN WHAT?
Implementation: What do I do?

How did Paul know that this church was worldly? The answer will help us evaluate our churches and our own personal lives to see if we also have characteristics of worldliness. Paul let this church know that they were worldly, not spiritual. In verse 3, he told them that their worldliness was demonstrated by their jealousy and quarreling. The believers had divided into cliques. Some bragged by saying that because they followed Paul, they were superior. Others said they followed Apollos, so they were superior. What they demonstrated was that their loyalties were to men, not to God. Their pride blinded them to the fact that it was God who provided someone to impact their lives, and He determined how it would be done. Is there this kind of jealousy and quarreling in your youth group or church? Are people fighting and choosing sides based on issues like the school they attend, what ministry they are involved with, or their preferences? If the answer is yes, your group is worldly. What can you do to keep yourself or your church from allowing this kind of worldliness to prevent spiritual growth and influence in your community? Are you willing to do it?

X**TRA READING**
1 CORINTHIANS 3

## PEOPLE OR GOD?

### 1 CORINTHIANS 4:1-5

How much do you care about what others think of you? Does someone's opinion of you affect the way you dress? Does it affect how you act? Are there times when you want to take a stand but do not because you are afraid of what people may think? It would be great if we could all say what Paul did in verse 3 of this chapter. The most important thing to Paul was that he be found faithful--but faithful by whose definition? According to verse 3, the only person he really cared to please was God. He did not care if the Corinthians or any other human court judged him critically. In fact, he did not even look at his own conscience to determine how faithful he was. His only concern was how God would judge him. Can you say the same thing? Do you live your life knowing you will stand before God one day and will be judged by His standard? Do you enter school or work with your only goal being to please God? The world needs Christians who will live their lives committed to God and pleasing Him alone. There are too many believers who care more about what people think than what God thinks. Are you one of them? How can that change?

### SAY WHAT?

How can you tell if you are someone who cares more about what people think than what God thinks?

### SO WHAT?

Why is this such a big issue in your life?

### NOW WHAT?

How can you begin changing your focus from what people think to what God thinks?

### THEN WHAT?

In light of this passage, what personal commitment can you make?

**XTRA READING**
1 CORINTHIANS 4

# 1 CORINTHIANS 5:1-8

## SAY WHAT?

Observation: What do I see?

## SO WHAT?

Interpretation: What does it mean?

## NOW WHAT?

Application: How does it apply to me?

## THEN WHAT?

Implementation: What do I do?

When was the last time you saw or heard about a church exercising church discipline? Why is it important for churches to make sure they exercise church discipline? What are the consequences if a church does not fulfill that responsibility? Paul answered those questions in today's reading. First, he told them church discipline is important for the restoration of the one who is in sin. According to verse 5, discipline provides the opportunity for his sinful nature to be destroyed and his spirit to be saved. If church discipline is used improperly or not at all, the person in sin loses an opportunity to be saved. We often think tolerance of sin is loving and kind, but if we don't practice discipline, we are really hurting the brother who is in sin. Second, according to verse 6, it keeps sin from spreading throughout the whole church. By ignoring sin, we allow the potential for it to spread and hurt others. There are some who see discipline as harsh actions towards those we love. God's Word takes a very different view. If we care about a person in sin and we care about the body of Christ, we will not only exercise Biblical discipline as a church, but also as individuals who truly care.

**XTRA READING**
1 CORINTHIANS 5

## DISPUTES

How should Christians settle disputes? If, for example, a believer owes another believer a large sum of money and it has caused problems between them, how should that be handled? Should the church get involved? The answer is in today's reading. Paul makes it very clear in this passage that Christians are to work to settle their disputes within the body of Christ. If a dispute arises, the Christians involved are to attempt to work it out themselves. If they are unable to come up with a solution, they then are to bring the matter to church leaders who have been selected to help in situations like these. Christians should never take a dispute out into public. In fact, Paul says it is better to be wronged or cheated than to have your dispute with another believer brought out in public. The reason? Because it is so damaging to the cause of Christ. The world looks at these disputes and wonders why two people, who claim to have Christ controlling their lives, can't settle a problem. Our testimony is more important than proving who's right or wrong in these kinds of matters. How can you apply this passage? Use today's questions to help you get started.

### SAY WHAT?

What disputes have you had with other Christians?

### SO WHAT?

How have they been resolved?

### NOW WHAT?

How should this passage impact the way you respond to disputes with other believers in the future?

### THEN WHAT?

In light of this passage, what personal commitment can you make?

**XTRA READING**

**1 CORINTHIANS 6**

## PROVERBS 24

The book of Proverbs was designed to help us in "attaining wisdom and discipline; in understanding words of insight; in acquiring a disciplined and prudent life, doing what is right and just and fair; in giving prudence to the simple, knowledge and discretion to the young." As you read through this chapter, write down the verses that are most significant to you in your present circumstances.

VERSE    |    WHAT TRUTH IT COMMUNICATES    |    HOW IT IMPACTS MY LIFE

## I, NOT THE LORD

### 1 CORINTHIANS 7:8-16

What does Paul mean by the phrase "I, not the Lord" in today's reading? Does he mean that what he said was his opinion and not directly from God? The answer could impact your view of how our Bible was written, and whether we can really trust it. Paul, in this section of Scripture, was giving us God's truth concerning marriage. First, he explains that marriage is the place God intended for sexual fulfillment. Sex outside of marriage violates God's plan and is sin. Second, when he talks about divorce, he adds the phrase, "not I, but the Lord," to show the readers that what he just stated had already been communicated in Scripture. The paragraph beginning with verse 12, covers an area in which God had not yet given a command. Therefore, Paul used the phrase, "I, not the Lord," to say this is a new command which God is revealing now through him. It was not to state that it was just Paul's opinion. It is God's truth given through Paul as he wrote this letter to the Corinthians. Remember, all Scripture is given by God and should be read and obeyed as such. We must therefore view verses 12-16 as God's specific communication.

### SAY WHAT?
Observation: What do I see?

### SO WHAT?
Interpretation: What does it mean?

### NOW WHAT?
Application: How does it apply to me?

### THEN WHAT?
Implementation: What do I do?

**XTRA READING**

1 CORINTHIANS 7

## 1 CORINTHIANS 8:1-13

### SAY WHAT?

What kinds of issues in today's Christianity are similar to eating sacrificed meat in Paul's day?

### SO WHAT?

Why do people have such different views about those issues?

### NOW WHAT?

How can today's passage help you know how to respond to these issues in the future?

### THEN WHAT?

In light of this passage, what personal commitment can you make?

How deeply do you care about other people? How badly do you want them to have a walk with God and avoid sin? Do you care enough to give up something you might enjoy in order to help them grow? You would if you cared as much as Paul did. There was a major dispute in this church when this letter was written. Some believers felt that it was acceptable to eat meat that had been sacrificed to idols. Weaker believers felt it was wrong. Paul's concern was not whether it was right or wrong, but how one's behavior would impact those weaker brothers around him. His priority was to be his concern for others. If a weaker brother was offended, he gladly gave up meat, even though eating it was not wrong. If eating meat could result in a weaker brother returning to a sinful past, he would gladly give it up forever. Why? He cared more about others than he did his own freedom. Can you say the same thing? Would you willingly give something up because a weaker brother felt it was wrong? At what level of personal cost would you draw the line of sacrifice? Use today's questions to help you think through and respond to this important principle.

**XTRA READING**
1 CORINTHIANS 8-9

## NEVERTHELESS

### 1 CORINTHIANS 10:1-13

What can you tell about your own spiritual condition by looking at your church or family? According to today's reading, maybe nothing. Paul tells us that, as a nation, the Israelites had seen God move on their behalf in powerful ways. They were all led by the same cloud, they all ate the same food, they all drank water from a rock, and they even had the very presence of Christ with them as they traveled. It would have been easy for a member of the nation of Israel to conclude he was spiritual because of what God had done for the Israelites. According to verse 5, however, God was not pleased with most of them. The majority of Israelites did not love God and were not committed to serving Him. In fact, most of them never made it to the Promised Land. Why not? Because they had no real personal relationship with Christ. Could you be like one of the Israelites? Is God moving in your church or your family and yet, He is not pleased with you? Being a part of a group where God is at work does not reveal where one stands personally before God. Examine the condition of your heart, not what is going on around you, to see where you truly stand.

**SAY WHAT?**
Observation: What do I see?

**SO WHAT?**
Interpretation: What does it mean?

**NOW WHAT?**
Application: How does it apply to me?

**THEN WHAT?**
Implementation: What do I do?

**XTRA READING**
1 CORINTHIANS 10

ocd

## 1 CORINTHIANS 11:17-34

### SAY WHAT?

In what ways is division evident in your church?

### SO WHAT?

In what ways is selfishness evident in your church?

### NOW WHAT?

How can you prevent selfishness and division from occurring in your church and in your life?

### THEN WHAT?

In light of this passage, what personal commitment can you make?

In what ways are meetings at your church similar to the meetings in this chapter? Unfortunately, the same characteristics we see in today's reading find their way into a lot of churches today. Paul was very discouraged with the behavior and the underlying motivations of the church at Corinth. When they came together, instead of being unified around their commitment to Christ and their desire to impact their world, they were divided. Paul tells them that disagreements were not only okay, but are actually necessary. The problem was not that there were disagreements, but that disagreements had led to people being disagreeable and causing division. They cared more about having their own needs met than worshiping God, which was why they were supposed to be at church in the first place. Even their communion service, the purpose of which was to remember Christ, had degenerated into simply a free meal. Do you see these characteristics in your church? How do they demonstrate themselves? What can you do to be sure you are not part of creating them? What can you do to prevent them from happening?

### XTRA READING

1 CORINTHIANS 11

## SPIRITUAL GIFTS-PART 1

As Paul began his discussion on spiritual gifts, what three important truths did he teach? Why did God have him begin this chapter with them? A close look will reveal the answers. First, in verse 4, Paul explained that there are different gifts, but the same Spirit gives these gifts. He wanted to communicate that not everyone will have the same gifts, nor should we want to. The Spirit decides who gets what gifts. Second, Paul teaches that there are different kinds of service, but Christ decides which service one has. Each of us has a specific job were we are to use the gift the Spirit has given to us. Though we might have the same gift as someone else, our job may be different. Third, Paul explains that there are different works, but it is the Father who determines what those works are. When we use our gifts to do our jobs, God brings about the results. Just as our gifts and jobs are determined by the Godhead, so are the results when we use them. We should not be jealous or envious of others' gifts, jobs, or results. Further, we ought to know what our gifts are so we can begin to use them. Do you? How are you using yours?

### SAY WHAT?

Observation: What do I see?

### SO WHAT?

Interpretation: What does it mean?

### NOW WHAT?

Application: How does it apply to me?

### THEN WHAT?

Implementation: What do I do?

**XTRA READING**
1 CORINTHIANS 12

## 1 CORINTHIANS 13:1-7

**LOVE**

| CHARACTERISTIC | HOW I DEMONSTRATE IT | HOW I CAN IMPROVE IT |
| --- | --- | --- |
| IS PATIENT | | |
| IS KIND | | |
| DOES NOT ENVY | | |
| DOES NOT BOAST | | |
| IS NOT PROUD | | |
| IS NOT RUDE | | |
| NOT SELF-SEEKING | | |
| IS NOT EASILY ANGERED | | |
| KEEPS NO RECORD OF WRONGS | | |
| DOES NOT DELIGHT IN EVIL | | |
| ALWAYS PROTECTS | | |
| ALWAYS TRUSTS | | |

This passage is often called the love chapter. We are given 12 characteristics of true love. Use the chart provided to help you examine your love and find ways to improve. Imagine what would happen if these 12 characteristics dominated your life or your church.

**XTRA READING**
1 CORINTHIANS 13

The book of Proverbs was designed to help us in "attaining wisdom and discipline; in understanding words of insight; in acquiring a disciplined and prudent life, doing what is right and just and fair; in giving prudence to the simple, knowledge and discretion to the young." As you read through this chapter, write down the verses that are most significant to you in your present circumstances.

VERSE | WHAT TRUTH IT COMMUNICATES | HOW IT IMPACTS MY LIFE

## 1 CORINTHIANS 14:1-12

## SPIRITUAL GIFTS-PART 2

### SAY WHAT?
Observation: What do I see?

### SO WHAT?
Interpretation: What does it mean?

### NOW WHAT?
Application: How does it apply to me?

### THEN WHAT?
Implementation: What do I do?

As chapter 14 continues with the subject of spiritual gifts, what new truths do we find? Because the church in Corinth had a misunderstanding of spiritual gifts and had misused them, Paul gave them more instructions in today's reading. First, they had determined that some spiritual gifts were more desirable than others, so they were trying to seek those gifts for themselves. They had forgotten that gifts were given by the Holy Spirit and were not something to request or seek. Second, their understanding of the purpose of spiritual gifts was wrong. As a result, their services had gotten out of hand and true worship was not even taking place. In fact, gifts they were attempting to use for themselves were really designed for the unsaved, not for personal worship or spiritual growth. As a result, Paul gave them specific information about gifts and how they were to be used. A misunderstanding of the gifts can lead to wrong doctrine and ineffective ministry. Do you have a proper understanding of spiritual gifts? What have you learned in the last three chapters to help you?

**X**TRA READING
1 CORINTHIANS 14

## PASSED ON

As you read this chapter, what thoughts came to your mind? Did you think about people in your world who do not know Christ? While this is possibly the greatest chapter in the Bible on the resurrection, there are two phrases that have a great impact on our view of outreach. In fact, when you connect them, they have an even greater impact. The first phrase is found in verse 3. Paul said that he passed on what he had received. In other words, he was given the truth of the Gospel and had passed it on so that others could know this truth and have their lives changed. The second phrase is found in verse 34. Here, Paul told them that there were some in Corinth who were ignorant of God. In other words, the people in the church of Corinth had not done what Paul did with the truth they received. Paul passed it on to others while, to the shame of this church, they had not. Could the same thing be said of you? You have been given great truth and opportunities, but have you passed it on? Is there someone in your world who is ignorant of the Gospel because you have not shared it? How can you correct that this week?

### SAY WHAT?
Observation: What do I see?

### SO WHAT?
Interpretation: What does it mean?

### NOW WHAT?
Application: How does it apply to me?

### THEN WHAT?
Implementation: What do I do?

**XTRA READING**
1 CORINTHIANS 15

## 1 CORINTHIANS 16:1-9

## OPPORTUNITY & OPPOSITION

### SAY WHAT?

In what ways have you been challenged by reading 1 Corinthians?

### SO WHAT?

What did you learn from reading 1 Corinthians?

### NOW WHAT?

How can you use these truths right now?

### THEN WHAT?

In light of this passage, what personal commitment can you make?

If you really began to walk with God and gain a burden to influence your world for Christ, what could you expect to happen? One part of the answer is encouraging, while the other part could be discouraging. The encouraging part is to know that when someone is truly walking with God and seeking to influence his world, God will use him to make a difference. In today's reading, we see that God had opened a great door for effective ministry in Ephesus. How exciting it must have been to be a part of this great work, watching God use them to influence people's lives. But, did you notice what else was taking place in Ephesus? Here is the discouraging part. According to verse 9, not only did Paul have an open door, but there were many who opposed him. It was not all fun and games. Likewise, when you begin to influence people for Christ, you will find opposition. We need to realize it will come and avoid being discouraged or deterred by it. Satan does not like to see people influenced for Christ and will attempt to do all he can to stop you. Stand firm and keep plugging away. See the opposition as evidence you are making a difference.

**XTRA READING**
1 CORINTHIANS 16

## POWER OF PRAYER

**2 CORINTHIANS 1:3-11**

How was it that Paul was able to endure the opposition in his life and still be faithful and committed to his call? Did he know something or do something we can use when we face hard times today? We find part of the answer in today's reading. It is an exciting aspect of our daily faith that we can all have a part in. Paul said, in verse 8, that there were times of extreme difficulty when they weren't sure that they would even live through it. Those events, however, enabled him to learn to trust in God and not in himself or his abilities. He then told the Corinthians that he would continue to serve God and trust Him to deliver them. Why? According to verse 11, it was because these Christians had been praying for Paul. Their prayers helped enable Paul to keep pressing on and to allow the difficult times to make him strong. This should motivate us to become more faithful in our prayers for others as they serve God. Prayer is an important tool of encouragement. We can help people endure difficult times, watch their dependence on God grow, and see godliness produced in their lives because we prayed for them. Who can you be praying for? Why not begin now?

**XTRA READING**

2 CORINTHIANS 1

### SAY WHAT?
Observation: What do I see?

### SO WHAT?
Interpretation: What does it mean?

### NOW WHAT?
Application: How does it apply to me?

### THEN WHAT?
Implementation: What do I do?

## 2 CORINTHIANS 2:12-17

## MOTIVATION

### SAY WHAT?

What kinds of motivations could you have for doing "spiritual" things?

### SO WHAT?

How can you tell what your motivation is for doing "spiritual" things?

### NOW WHAT?

How can you ensure that pure motives are part of your walk with God?

### THEN WHAT?

In light of this passage, what personal commitment can you make?

What is your motivation for serving God? Why do you have devotions? Why do you serve in the church? Why do you even go to church? Often, people do these very good and right things for the wrong reasons. People have their devotions because they want others to think they are spiritual. Some serve in the church so that positive things will be said about them. In today's reading, we learn what motivated the Apostle Paul to do these things. According to verse 17, it was not for money, but out of sincerity. He had the words of truth that could transform people's lives. He knew firsthand what power those words had. Paul knew that some served God for what they could get out of it. Some even served for the money they could make. Paul, however, was different. He was a man sent by God to accomplish something very specific and important on this earth. What other motivation could he have to serve? Why not examine your own life and ask yourself what motivates you to do the spiritual things you do? We should never serve God because of personal gain or selfishness, but as people sent by God to help others. Use today's questions to get started.

### XTRA READING
2 CORINTHIANS 2

## BEING TRANSFORMED                    2 CORINTHIANS 3:7-18

How is your walk with God different today than it was a year ago? Would you say you are growing spiritually? Would you say that you are stronger in your faith now than you were one year ago? Has your knowledge of God and His Word grown since last winter? Could you describe your walk with God the way Paul did in verse 18 of today's reading? Paul said that he was a man who reflected the glory of God. He was a man who was "being" transformed into the likeness of Christ. He was "becoming" more like Christ every day. Each day, more of the glory of God was evident in his life. That must have been exciting for him! To look back on your life and see how God has transformed you into the likeness of Christ is something to get excited about. On the other hand, little or no growth ought to discourage us. God intended for each of us to grow in our walk with Him. It is not His desire for us to be at a spiritual standstill. We, like Paul, ought to be becoming more like Christ each day. Are you? In what ways have you grown in your walk with God? Are you "being" transformed to display His glory to the people you see every day? Use today's questions to get started.

### SAY WHAT?

In what area have you seen spiritual growth since school started this fall?

### SO WHAT?

How are you more like Christ now than you were last Fall?

### NOW WHAT?

What do you need to do in order to see continued growth this next year? Who can help you create a specific plan?

### THEN WHAT?

In light of this passage, what personal commitment can you make?

**XTRA READING**
2 CORINTHIANS 3

## PROVERBS 26

The book of Proverbs was designed to help us in "attaining wisdom and discipline; in understanding words of insight; in acquiring a disciplined and prudent life, doing what is right and just and fair; in giving prudence to the simple, knowledge and discretion to the young." As you read through this chapter, write down the verses that are most significant to you in your present circumstances.

VERSE   |   WHAT TRUTH IT COMMUNICATES   |   HOW IT IMPACTS MY LIFE

## PRIORITIES

### 2 CORINTHIANS 4:7-18

In today's reading, we learn three important priorities we ought to have as Christians. They are given to us in verses 16-18. Did you notice them? Mark them in your Bible. First, we are to view the spiritual as more important than the physical. We must realize that what happens to us physically results in spiritual growth. If we care more about spiritual growth than physical comfort, we will rejoice when trouble strikes. Second, we are to view the future as having greater importance than the present. Paul did not mean in verse 17 that the present does not matter or that its problems shouldn't be a concern. He meant that, in the midst of our present problems, we should realize that they are achieving for us something greater for the future. Therefore, since we are more concerned about the future than the present, we rejoice. Third, we are to view the eternal as more important than the temporal. God, Christ, and the souls of men are more important than jobs, grades, awards, money, prestige, or anything else that won't be with us in eternity. Would your life be characterized by these three priorities? Use today's questions to help you do honest evaluation about your priorities.

### SAY WHAT?

How would someone act who views physical comfort as more important than spiritual growth?

### SO WHAT?

How would someone act who views the present as more important than the future?

### NOW WHAT?

How would someone act who views the temporal as more important than the eternal?

### THEN WHAT?

In light of this passage, what personal commitment can you make?

XTRA READING
2 CORINTHIANS 4

## 2 CORINTHIANS 5:11-21

## CHRIST'S AMBASSADORS

### SAY WHAT?

Observation: What do I see?

### SO WHAT?

Interpretation: What does it mean?

### NOW WHAT?

Application: How does it apply to me?

### THEN WHAT?

Implementation: What do I do?

What responsibility do those of us who have received Jesus Christ have to the rest of the world? How does your answer to that question impact how you live your life? The answer is found in today's reading. Paul reminds the Corinthians that they have been reconciled to God. This means that they have had their debt of sin paid for and have received eternal life. He reminds them that they have been made new. According to verse 16, as a result, their view of the world ought to have changed. Since they have been reconciled, God has given to them the ministry of reconciliation for the world. That is, they have become God's ambassadors. God is, in fact, making His appeal to the world through we who have been reconciled. What an awesome responsibility! He has given us the message of reconciliation to share with those who don't know or understand what reconciliation is. We need to tell people that they can be right with God and have a relationship with Him. He can change lives and we are the living proof. How well are you fulfilling your responsibility? Can you name someone with whom you recently shared God's plan of salvation? Better get started!

### XTRA READING

2 CORINTHIANS 5

## IN VAIN

## 2 CORINTHIANS 6:1-13

Verse 1 of this chapter tells us not to receive the grace of God in vain. What does that mean and how do we do it? This is an important question that Christians don't seem to take time to consider. To answer it, we must look closely at the context. While our Bibles have a chapter division here, Paul's original letter did not. It is obvious that he was continuing his thoughts and discussion from chapter 5. He concluded that chapter with the discussion of our salvation and our ministry of reconciliation. Therefore, according to the context, we receive the grace of God in vain when we do not fulfill our ministry of reconciliation. We receive the grace of God in vain when we accept our salvation but then keep it to ourselves. We receive the grace of God in vain when we isolate ourselves in the safe world of Christianity and fail to reach a lost world with the message of Christ. If you have not been actively sharing your faith and the message that everyone can be reconciled to God, you have received the grace of God in vain. It is a tragedy to have what the world needs and neglect to share the message. So, have you received the grace of God in vain?

### SAY WHAT?

In what ways have you seen people receive the grace of God in vain?

### SO WHAT?

In what ways have you received the grace of God in vain?

### NOW WHAT?

How can you avoid being one who receives God's grace in vain?

### THEN WHAT?

In light of this passage, what personal commitment can you make?

XTRA READING

2 CORINTHIANS 6

## 2 CORINTHIANS 7:8-16

## COMPLETE CONFIDENCE

### SAY WHAT?

Observation: What do I see?

### SO WHAT?

Interpretation: What does it mean?

### NOW WHAT?

Application: How does it apply to me?

### THEN WHAT?

Implementation: What do I do?

In this chapter, Paul has written some amazing things about the church in Corinth. Look at verse 16. Could those who know you say that about your life? Paul wrote in this letter how thrilled he was with the report Titus gave him concerning their lives. They continued to be loyal to Paul. They repented of the sin they had committed and demonstrated their repentance with godly sorrow. Paul had great love for and pride in these people, and Titus saw why after spending time with them. Their love for God and commitment to Him was a source of joy for Paul. He told Titus that they were a great group of believers, and he would have a wonderful time with them. Titus returned to Paul encouraged and refreshed by this church. It would have humiliated Paul to find out after Titus returned that this church did not live up to the expectation Paul had for them. His words could have caused great embarrassment for him, but they didn't. Could the same thing be said of you or your church? If someone were to see who you are in all areas of your life, would you be an embarrassment or an encouragement to them? Is the life you live publically who you really are?

X**TRA READING**
2 CORINTHIANS 7

## GIVING

How well are you doing in the area of giving? How much money have you given to your church this year? Is there a Biblical method we can use to evaluate ourselves honestly in this area? Paul answers that question in today's reading. The answer, however, may not be an encouragement to some of us. In this chaper, Paul teaches us what our motivation for giving ought to be and whose example we are to follow. First, we learn that the example we are to follow in our giving is Jesus Christ's. Although He was rich, He was willing to become poor for us. He gave everything He had for us. Often, we give out of our surplus or in ways that do not cost us anything. What have you sacrificed in order to give to your church or to someone in need? Second, we are to give because we want to help others become rich. It is out of love and concern for others that we make sacrifices. Have you recently made a sacrifice in order to provide for the needs of others? How does your life compare to the standard set by Jesus? Remember, He is our example. Although He was rich, He was willing to become poor out of His great love for you and me. Is your giving like that?

### SAY WHAT?

Observation: What do I see?

### SO WHAT?

Interpretation: What does it mean?

### NOW WHAT?

Application: How does it apply to me?

### THEN WHAT?

Implementation: What do I do?

**XTRA READING**

2 CORINTHIANS 8

## 2 CORINTHIANS 10:1-6

**WEAPONS**

### SAY WHAT?

What are some of the weapons the world uses to fight battles?

### SO WHAT?

Which of the world's weapons do you find yourself using the most?

### NOW WHAT?

How can you begin training yourself to use the weapons of God and not the weapons of the world?

### THEN WHAT?

In light of this passage, what personal commitment can you make?

When was the last time you faced opposition because of your faith? When someone opposes you or disagrees with a Biblical standard, how should you respond? According to today's reading, your response should be radically different than a non-believer's. Paul tells us that the weapons the world uses are not the weapons Christians use. The world's weapons do not have divine power and are not able to truly demolish strongholds. Our weapons as Christians, however, are different. They have divine power and are able to demolish arguments and break through the hearts of people. They are prayer, the Word of God, and changed lives. When we are facing opposition, why would we fight with the weapons the world uses and not use the ones God has given to us? Why do we think it is better to debate or convince people with our clever arguments when we can get down on our knees and pray? That logic is from the world. Are you using God's weapons in your battle? How can you become more effective in using the weapons God has given to us?

**XTRA READING**
2 CORINTHIANS 9, 10

## ANGEL OF LIGHT

What is Satan's agenda for our lives? According to 1 Peter 5:8, it is to destroy us. But how does he try to do it? According to today's reading, he comes as an angel of light. In other words, he deceives us by appearing harmless and innocent. In fact, sometimes it is very difficult to see that it really is Satan trying to destroy us and not something good. Sometimes people who seem as if they have our best interest in mind are actually being used by Satan to try to defeat us. Certain kinds of activities may not appear to be harmful, but eventually lead us down a road to great sin and destruction. If Satan's plans were obvious, we would run for cover. He hides evil behind the appearance of good or in a neutral area. We then walk down the road, blind to what is actually going on. Could you be involved in something right now that seems to be okay but is, in fact, Satan's deception? It could be TV programs that seem okay but, in reality, are weakening your ability to resist sin. It may be a friendship you have developed that will ultimately encourage you to sin. Ask God to open your eyes to see the reality of Satan's attacks.

### SAY WHAT?
Observation: What do I see?

### SO WHAT?
Interpretation: What does it mean?

### NOW WHAT?
Application: How does it apply to me?

### THEN WHAT?
Implementation: What do I do?

**X TRA READING**
2 CORINTHIANS 11

## 2 CORINTHIANS 12:1-10

### SAY WHAT?

In telling the stories of our lives, how do we give ourselves the glory?

### SO WHAT?

Why is it so difficult for us to rejoice in times of suffering?

### NOW WHAT?

How can you live to bring glory to God and not to yourself?

### THEN WHAT?

In light of this passage, what personal commitment can you make?

Are there accomplishments in your life that you are proud of and enjoy discussing with friends? Would they be the same items Paul mentioned in this chapter? Notice what Paul listed in verses 9 and 10. Paul boasted about his weaknesses. He did not talk about the things he did well, but about those things he did not do well. He not only spoke of his weaknesses, but joyfully endured insults, hardships, persecutions, and difficulties. Why? Look at verse 10. When he was weak, God made him strong. He boasted about his weaknesses because he could see God in them. When he was insulted and persecuted, God gave him strength to endure. When he faced difficulties and hardships, God energized him to persevere. God wants us to be totally dependent on Him, too. He wants all the glory to go to His Name. We often operate in our own strength, depend on ourselves to persevere, and then give ourselves the glory. We resist difficult times and forget that it is in the painful moments that God makes us more like Christ. Who receives glory for what is accomplished in your life? What do your stories tell?

### XTRA READING

2 CORINTHIANS 12

## WHO IS PAUL?

### 2 CORINTHIANS 13:1-10

What have you learned about the Apostle Paul after reading through this book? If the only source of information you had was this book, what conclusion would you make about his life? We could describe him as a man who deeply loved the church in Corinth. He wanted them to be all God made them to be. When someone tried to malign Paul's ministry in the church, his response was governed by their best interest, not his reputation. He took a stand for what was right and loved them enough to tell them what was right, even though it may have been difficult for them to hear and may have caused pain among them. He closed this letter by again showing his deep love for these people. He asked them to honestly look at their lives and evaluate the condition of their hearts. Finally, he told them not to settle for anything but perfection. It is wonderful to have someone in your life who cares for you like this. At times, they may make you uncomfortable, but they enable you to keep on track in your walk with God. Why not finish this book by reflecting on who those people are in your life. Thank them for their love and concern even when it makes you angry or uncomfortable.

**SAY WHAT?**
Observation: What do I see?

**SO WHAT?**
Interpretation: What does it mean?

**NOW WHAT?**
Application: How does it apply to me?

**THEN WHAT?**
Implementation: What do I do?

**XTRA READING**
2 CORINTHIANS 13

OCD

CHRIST HAS LIBERATED US TO BE FREE.
STAND FIRM THEN AND DON'T SUBMIT AGAIN
TO A YOKE OF SLAVERY.
GALATIANS 5:1

# SET
# FREE

ontrack devotions

**FEBRUARY**

2017

GALATIANS
EPHESIANS
PHILIPPIANS
COLOSSIANS

# MONTHLY PRAYER SHEET

"...The prayer of a righteous man is powerful and effective." James 5:16

| Reach out... | How I will do it... | How it went... |
|---|---|---|
|  |  |  |

| Other requests... | Answered | How it was answered... |
|---|---|---|
|  |  |  |

**Name:** _____

This sheet is designed to help you make personal commitments each month that will help you grow in your walk with God. Fill it out by determining
   1. What will push you
   2. What you think you can achieve
If you need help filling out your commitments, seek out someone you trust who can help you. Share your commitments with those who will help keep you accountable to your personal commitment.

## Personal Devotions:
How did I do with my commitment last month? _____
I will commit to read the OnTrack Bible passage and devotional thought _____ day(s) each week this month.

## Church Attendance:
How did I do last month with my attendance? _____
I will attend Youth/Growth Group_____ time(s) this month.
I will attend the Sunday AM service _____ time(s) this month.
I will attend the Sunday PM service_____ time(s) this month.
I will attend_____ time(s) this month.
I will attend_____ time(s) this month.

## Scripture Memory:
How did I do with Scripture memory last month? _____
I will memorize_____ key verse(s) from the daily OnTrack Devotions this month.

## Outreach:
How did I do last month with sharing Christ? _____
I will share Christ with _____ person/people this month.
I will serve my local church this month by _____
_____

## Other Activities:
List any other opportunities such as events, prayer group, etc., that you will participate in this month. _____
_____

## MOTIVE AND MESSAGE

How can you tell if someone is a true servant of Christ? How can you know if you are a true servant of Christ or simply a religious person? The answer is found in today's reading. Paul wrote this letter to refute incorrect teaching the church in Galatia was receiving. After Paul left for another region, someone began teaching wrong doctrine. How could the believers in this church identify who was speaking the truth? First, by examining the motives of the teachers. Paul's goal was to please God and not men (vs10). Unlike other teachers, his words were not motivated by gaining the approval or acceptance of these people. Second, by closely examining the message. Paul's message did not come from his personal experiences, his own ideas, or from someone else who taught him. His message came from God. Therefore, he could be trusted and his message could be believed. Likewise today, a true servant of God is characterized by right motives and a right message. What is your motive and message? Is your life about love for others or yourself? Is your message about how people can gain eternal life? Use today's questions to take a closer look.

### SAY WHAT?
How can you tell what someone's true motivation is?

### SO WHAT?
How can you tell if someone's message is correct?

### NOW WHAT?
In what ways do you demonstrate yourself to be someone who is a servant of God?

### THEN WHAT?
In light of this passage, what personal commitment can you make?

**XTRA READING**
GALATIANS 1

## SAY WHAT?
Observation: What do I see?

## SO WHAT?
Interpretation: What does it mean?

## NOW WHAT?
Application: How does it apply to me?

## THEN WHAT?
Implementation: What do I do?

We learned yesterday what motivated Paul. What did today's chapter reveal to you about the motivation of false teachers? If we look closely, we see they wanted to take away freedom in Christ and make people slaves to them (vs 4). These teachers wanted the believers to depend on them to identify what was right and what was wrong. Paul was different. He wanted these people to know and depend on God's Word and the Holy Spirit to lead and guide them. Paul wanted these believers to develop a relationship with God and learn to be sensitive to the leading of the Holy Spirit. Paul's desire was to help them know Christ and learn to depend on God and His Word, not on him. What kind of believer are you becoming? Do you study the Scriptures for yourself so that you know what they say and can make decisions guided by the Holy Spirit? Are you dependent on others to tell you what is right and wrong? Are you spending time each day developing your relationship with God and His Word? Commit yourself to developing these skills and allowing the godly leadership in your life to help you along the way.

**X**TRA READING
GALATIANS 2

## OUR SALVATION

Throughout his letter, Paul gave proof to the Galatians that trying to earn salvation and grow spiritually by following the Law was wrong. In today's reading, he gave them another example of how faulty the information from some of their leaders was. Did you notice it as you read these verses? Paul asked each of them to examine their lives in order to determine what to believe. Paul had clearly communicated the message of the Gospel to them. They knew that Jesus had died to pay for their sins. They knew that the requirements were trusting Christ and accepting the salvation He offered by faith. They were justified by faith because they believed what they heard. Paul's example of Abraham further illustrated this truth. Take a look at your own life. Has your life changed since you trusted Christ? Did it change because you followed a religious system of good works? No! It changed when you trusted Christ. This is the message we must take to the world. We need to let people know that salvation and change comes not from doing good works, but by the work of Christ. Are you telling them? Does your life support your message?

### SAY WHAT?

What were the circumstances that led to your salvation? Where were you? Why did you trust Christ?

### SO WHAT?

In what ways has your life changed since that point?

### NOW WHAT?

In what ways can you share the truth that you have already discovered?

### THEN WHAT?

In light of this passage, what personal commitment can you make?

XTRA READING
GALATIANS 3

## GALATIANS 3:15-29

### SAY WHAT?

Observation: What do I see?

### SO WHAT?

Interpretation: What does it mean?

### NOW WHAT?

Application: How does it apply to me?

### THEN WHAT?

Implementation: What do I do?

If following the Law or doing works does not bring about transformation or a right relationship with God, what was the purpose of the Law that God gave to Moses? According to verse 24, it was given to bring us to Christ. Christ is our only means of becoming righteous. The Law cannot make us righteous. The purpose of the Law was to reveal one's need of a Savior. It shows us that it is not possible to earn one's way to heaven through doing good works. It is a standard that is too high for any human to achieve. The Law shows us our need for another way to gain access to God. It demonstrates our sinfulness and ultimately leads us to the Savior. The Law enables us to see that the only way we can gain access to God is through faith in Jesus Christ. Through Him we become sons of God. We are not slaves who follow a system in order to gain favor. We are sons who have gained our sonship through our new birth into the family of God. Without a standard (the Law), we would not know how short we have fallen or how much help we need. There are so many people who are trying to earn their way to God and don't realize that Jesus Christ has already done the work. Are you letting them know?

**XTRA READING**
GALATIANS 3

The book of Proverbs was designed to help us in "attaining wisdom and discipline; in understanding words of insight; in acquiring a disciplined and prudent life, doing what is right and just and fair; in giving prudence to the simple, knowledge and discretion to the young." As you read through this chapter, write down the verses that are most significant to you in your present circumstances.

VERSE | WHAT TRUTH IT COMMUNICATES | HOW IT IMPACTS MY LIFE

## GALATIANS 4:8-20

### SAY WHAT?

Name a couple of people who have invested time and energy into your life?

### SO WHAT?

In what ways have they impacted your life?

### NOW WHAT?

How can you demonstrate to them that their efforts have not been in vain?

### THEN WHAT?

In light of this passage, what personal commitment can you make?

Think of an individual or two who have invested time and effort in your life to help you grow in your walk with God. As they evaluate your spiritual journey to this point, how do you think they feel about the time and effort they have devoted to your life? Paul, in verse 11 of today's reading, makes a statement that ought to cause us to think about this very question. He invested a lot of time in the lives of the believers in the church of Galatia. Most of his time was devoted to studying the Word, teaching it carefully, and trying to build relationships with them to help them grow spiritually. If they began to fall away and believe the false teachers, he feared his effort would have been in vain. Had the Galatians ignored the truth and lived as though they had never heard it, Paul's many hours of patient teaching would have been for nothing. It is discouraging to work to ensure that one knows the truth and how to apply it, only to see them disregard it by word or deed. It must break the hearts of parents, pastors, and friends who try diligently to help us, only to see the truth rejected. As they examine your life, how do you think they feel about where you are now?

**XTRA READING**

GALATIANS 4

## FAITH ALONE

Today we learn in more detail about what the false teachers were actually teaching and how it influenced this church. According to verses 2-3, the false teachers were instructing them to be circumcised and follow the Law in order to become righteous and know for certain that they were saved. They had eliminated faith from salvation and made it works-based instead. If one believes that in order to be saved he must follow certain rules, his belief actually denies that faith in Christ alone is enough to save him. He also would conclude that what Jesus did on the cross helps, but it is not sufficient to get one to heaven. Another logical conclusion he would make is that it is also his responsibility to live a righteous life to ensure favor with God. What Jesus Christ did on the cross is all we need to get to heaven. We cannot earn it, nor do we need to add to it. It is all we need. When we trust Christ, we become His sons and serve Him from hearts of love and gratitude. We do not earn His love or acceptance. He gives it to us when we trust Christ. How much more should we desire to give Him? Is that what motivates your life? Is your heart filled with gratitude? How is that gratitude demonstrated?

### SAY WHAT?
Observation: What do I see?

### SO WHAT?
Interpretation: What does it mean?

### NOW WHAT?
Application: How does it apply to me?

### THEN WHAT?
Implementation: What do I do?

**XTRA READING**

GALATIANS 5

OGd

## GALATIANS 5:13-26

## FRUIT, NOT WORKS

### SAY WHAT?

How are the acts of the sinful nature demonstrated in my life? (5:19-21)

### SO WHAT?

In what ways do I see the fruit of the Spirit in my life? (5:22-26)

### NOW WHAT?

What can I do to diminish the acts of the sinful nature and increase the fruit of the Spirit in my life?

### THEN WHAT?

What personal commitment can I make in light of today's reading?

If our actions cannot gain us favor with God and we are not to live according to lists of right and wrong, can we do whatever we want once we are saved? Not according to Paul. Paul writes that we are not to live by lists, but by the Spirit. He realizes that it could be possible for some to interpret his statements as a license to do wrong. They could use their freedom in Christ to do what their sinful nature wants to do, and then justify their behavior because, as believers, they are free from restrictive laws. Paul wrote to correct that reasoning that some were living by. Instead, they were to fulfill the principle of Scripture, "love your neighbor as yourself," while being guided by the Holy Spirit. We need to learn what the principles of Scripture are, and then allow the Holy Spirit to lead us to live accordingly. We, as believers, live by Biblical principles implemented by the guidance of the Holy Spirit. We do not live by a list of rules from men. How are you doing in this area? Are you successfully living by the Holy Spirit? Use today's questions to help you determine the steps you need to take to increase your dependence on the Holy Spirit.

**XTRA READING**

GALATIANS 5

## ESPECIALLY

How important are fellow Christians to you? Are they a high priority in your life? Is your commitment and care for your saved friends greater than your commitment to your unsaved friends? Paul finishes today with an interesting phrase that we could easily overlook. It is found in verse 10. His closing admonitions to the Galatians were to be careful of the false teachers, to be careful what is sown, and not to become weary in doing good. He then closed his letter encouraging them to take every opportunity available to do good to all people. Then he added the phrase, "especially to those who belong to the family of believers." In other words, it is more important for us to take advantage of every opportunity to do good to our brothers and sisters in Christ than it is to those who are not saved. Other believers ought to be the priority of our lives. We ought to care for each other and seek always to meet each other's needs because of our relationship to each other through Christ. Does your life reflect this priority? In what ways have you demonstrated love to the family of believers recently? How can you get started today?

### SAY WHAT?
Observation: What do I see?

### SO WHAT?
Interpretation: What does it mean?

### NOW WHAT?
Application: How does it apply to me?

### THEN WHAT?
Implementation: What do I do?

XTRA READING
GALATIANS 6

## EPHESIANS 1:15-23

### SAY WHAT?

How would you describe your prayer life for other believers?

### SO WHAT?

Why did you use those specific words to describe your prayer life in the first question?

### NOW WHAT?

What would you need to change in your prayer life for other believers in order to be able to say what Paul did?

### THEN WHAT?

In light of this passage, what personal commitment can you make?

What motivates you to pray for people? What motivated the Apostle Paul to pray for the believers in the church at Ephesus? The answer is found in verse 15 of today's reading. In verses 1-14, Paul listed spiritual blessings of believers and praised God for them. In fact, the first three chapters of Ephesians list incredible facts that characterize the lives of everyone who knows Christ as Savior. In this chapter, we find three of these truths. First, we learn that we are chosen. Second, that God predestined us to be adopted. Third, that we are saved because the message of the Gospel was made known to us. It is even more incredible that, at the moment of salvation, we were sealed with the Holy Spirit by God, which guarantees we can never lose our salvation. Paul thanked God every time he thought of these people and prayed for their continued spiritual growth. He wanted them to know God more, and have greater hope and power in their lives. Since this is also true of your saved friends, do you pray for them in the same way Paul did the Ephesians? Today would be a good day to get started doing just that.

**XTRA READING**

EPHESIANS 1

### BUT...

Have you ever noticed when you read Scripture how a small, seemingly insignificant word can be of such great importance? Today, we see one of those words in verse 4. Did you notice it? In verses 1-3, Paul described what our lives were like before we trusted Christ. He wrote that we were dead in our sin and were without hope. In fact, we could not help ourselves and had no hope of changing because we were dead. Then that key word "BUT." If that word was not included, the following 6 verses would not be possible. While it is true we were once dead in our sin, God graciously provided life for us because of His great love. He made the means of eternal life available to those who believe what He said. As a result, we now are alive in Him. But, do not miss the purpose for our salvation found in verse 10. God did this for us to be able to perform the good works He prepared in advance for us to do. God did not give you this life just to prevent you from spending eternity in hell. He saved you to accomplish something very specific on earth today. Do you know what He expects you to be doing right now? Are you doing it? Better get started.

**SAY WHAT?**

Observation: What do I see?

**SO WHAT?**

Interpretation: What does it mean?

**NOW WHAT?**

Application: How does it apply to me?

**THEN WHAT?**

Implementation: What do I do?

**XTRA READING**

EPHESIANS 2

## PROVERBS 28

The book of Proverbs was designed to help us in "attaining wisdom and discipline; in understanding words of insight; in acquiring a disciplined and prudent life, doing what is right and just and fair; in giving prudence to the simple, knowledge and discretion to the young." As you read through this chapter, write down the verses that are most significant to you in your present circumstances.

VERSE    |    WHAT TRUTH IT COMMUNICATES    |    HOW IT IMPACTS MY LIFE

Why is it true that so few Christians actually experience all God has for their lives? It may be that they have not understood or followed the steps Paul gives in the prayer found in this chapter. To be able to experience all God has provided, you must be strengthened in your inner man. There is no quick or easy way to strengthen your inner man. You simply must be committed to daily devotions, prayer, and Scripture memory over a long period of time. Second, as your inner man is strengthened, Christ will be comfortable and at home in your heart. Instead of having to clean house due to the sin He finds there, He can relax and enjoy your company. Third, when Christ begins to be at home in your life, you gain the power to understand the love of God and to know it experientially in your life. Finally, you then begin to see yourself becoming more and more like Christ. When this process is fulfilled, verse 20 becomes a reality. All of these characteristics build upon the previous one and are not independent of each other. They are intertwined. Pick the one you need to work on and get started today. Your life will never be the same.

### SAY WHAT?

How can you begin to strengthen your inner man?

### SO WHAT?

What area of your life needs to change in order for Christ to dwell comfortably?

### NOW WHAT?

How can you allow the love of God to dominate your life?

### THEN WHAT?

How can you allow the power of God to function in your life?

**XTRA READING**
EPHESIANS 3

## EPHESIANS 4:1-16

## SAY WHAT?

Observation: What do I see?

## SO WHAT?

Interpretation: What does it mean?

## NOW WHAT?

Application: How does it apply to me?

## THEN WHAT?

Implementation: What do I do?

What is the grace that is spoken about in verse 7? How does the answer impact our understanding of this passage? As we read the text and look at other passages of Scripture, we find that the grace Paul referred to here is our spiritual gifts. These gifts were given when we trusted Christ. In fact, when we understand Paul's meaning here, what follows is even more significant. Paul explains that God, in grace, has given each believer a spiritual gift(s). The gift(s) we receive is determined by Christ. There is nothing we can do to change the gift given to us. God has appointed pastors to help us use and develop our gifts. In fact, a pastor's job is to prepare us to use the gifts we were given in the areas of service God desires. When we use what we have been given in the way God has intended, the body of Christ is built up. Then, we will no longer be tossed back and forth, but will be sure of what we believe. What gift(s) has God given to you? In what way does God want you to use them? Are you developing and using what you've been given? Your pastor can help you get started.

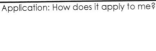

XTRA READING
EPHESIANS 4

## A PROCESS

Have you ever known of someone whose behavior is such that you wonder if he has any conscience at all? How can someone continually choose sin? How can a person get to this point in his life? According to today's passage, it involves a process, and it does not happen overnight. First, this person becomes darkened in his understanding. He does not allow the light of God in his life and loses any ability to clearly understand the truth. This lack of understanding leads him to be separated from God. God has no place in his life and he deliberately shuts Him out. Why? His heart has become hardened due to his ignorance. When all of this takes place, he loses all sensitivity and indulges in every kind of sexual sin. He does not, however, find any satisfaction and continually indulges. When someone chooses to shut God out, he begins walking a road that leads to behavior that today seems impossible. We must carefully guard our hearts and minds to prevent any movement away from God. How are you protecting yourself from this process? Use today's questions to help you build a strategy to ensure you do not take that first step.

### SAY WHAT?

How can you protect yourself from becoming darkened in your understanding?

### SO WHAT?

How can you protect yourself from becoming separated from God?

### NOW WHAT?

How can you protect yourself from developing a hardened heart?

### THEN WHAT?

In light of this passage, what personal commitment can you make?

### XTRA READING

EPHESIANS 4

**OCD**

 #ONTRACKDEVOS

## EPHESIANS 5:1-21                                            A HINT

### SAY WHAT?
Observation: What do I see?

### SO WHAT?
Interpretation: What does it mean?

### NOW WHAT?
Application: How does it apply to me?

### THEN WHAT?
Implementation: What do I do?

What would the definition of a "hint" of something be? What kinds of behavior would fall into this category? We would all agree that a "hint" of something is a very small amount. With that in mind, Paul's use of the word in today's reading is very important. He tells us that there must not be even a "hint" of sexual immorality, of any kind of impurity, or of greed. This is an indisputable expectation or standard. He did not expect that we would compare ourselves to others or evaluate our behavior based on another's wrongdoing. He did not say to end behavior that will lead us across the line of sin. He said that there should not even be a "hint" of those things--no trace of them in our lives. In verse 12, he said that it is shameful to even mention what the disobedient do in secret. This is a pretty high standard--no obscenity, no foolish talk, and no coarse joking. We are God's people and need to act like it. We are called to a higher standard than others. As you examine your own life, how do you measure up to this standard? What specific areas fall short? What needs to change to make sure there is not even a "hint?"

**XTRA READING**
EPHESIANS 5

## FUTURE HUSBANDS

**EPHESIANS 5:22-33**

How can you tell if the guy you are dating would be a godly husband? Is there any way we can know while dating? You can use today's reading as a guide. Paul gives four kinds of love husbands are to demonstrate. Girls can use this standard to see if, in their dating relationships, the guy measures up. First, husbands are to have sacrificial love (vs 25). In dating relationships, a guy demonstrates this kind of love by not always wanting his own way, only going where he wants, or hanging out with only his friends. Second, husbands are to demonstrate purifying love (vs 26-27). In dating, a guy would demonstrate this by seeking your purity as his priority. He would never ask you to violate your parents' standards or Scripture's commands. Third, husbands are to demonstrate caring love (vs 28-29). In dating, he is not harsh, mean, or unkind. Fourth, they are to demonstrate unbreakable love (vs 31). In dating, he is loyal to his family, friends, and his God. Use today's questions to help identify what characteristics to look for in a guy. Guys, use them to see what characteristics to develop as a future husband.

### SAY WHAT?

In what ways would a guy demonstrate sacrificial love?

### SO WHAT?

In what ways would a guy demonstrate purifying love?

### NOW WHAT?

In what ways would a guy demonstrate caring love?

### THEN WHAT?

In what ways would a guy demonstrate unbreakable love?

**XTRA READING**

EPHESIANS 5

## EPHESIANS 6:10-20

### SAY WHAT?

Observation: What do I see?

### SO WHAT?

Interpretation: What does it mean?

### NOW WHAT?

Application: How does it apply to me?

### THEN WHAT?

Implementation: What do I do?

As Christians, who is our enemy? Who is it that we are fighting? Today's reading reminds us who we are fighting and how to win the battle against our enemy. Verse 12 states that our battle is not with people, but with the forces of hell. Our parents, friends, teachers, or any authorities in our lives are not the enemy we battle against. We struggle against spiritual forces who are working against us. How do we fight these battles? We must use the armor that Paul describes for us in verses 14-18. Each piece is designed to help us successfully fight spiritual battles. Verse 18 mentions an often overlooked addition to the armor listed in this passage. It is prayer! We are told that we need to pray on ALL occasions with ALL kinds of prayers and requests. Too often, we fight, struggle, and try to fix our problems, never taking them to God in prayer. Prayer is one of the most valuable tools we have to fight and win in our spiritual battles. Unfortunately, we save prayer as a last resort or, worse yet, don't pray at all. How often are you using this weapon? What battle are you fighting that you need to pray about right now? Why not get started?

**XTRA READING**

EPHESIANS 6

# BIG PICTURE

How could Paul continue to rejoice in the situation in which he found himself? He was in chains, but yet, at peace. Can we find the same strength Paul did when we face difficult times? We can if we learn to have a "big picture" perspective like he did. Paul refused to concentrate on current circumstances. He saw the big picture and realized that God was accomplishing great things, even if he was personally uncomfortable. He was in chains, but the whole palace guard heard the message of the Gospel because of Paul's circumstances. He was in prison but, due to his suffering, many brothers in Christ had the courage to speak out for Him. His suffering was intentionally made worse, but more people than ever were hearing the Gospel message. Paul knew that God was in control, and while the small picture outlook was bleak, the big picture was moving the way God was directing. Paul could rejoice because God was being glorified. Is this your perspective? Are you focusing on the small picture of your present circumstances and how they affect you? What could the big picture be? Use today's questions to help you.

## SAY WHAT?

What kinds of things in our lives discourage us even though they are "small picture" circumstances?

## SO WHAT?

What are the "big picture" things God is working to accomplish in those areas?

## NOW WHAT?

What can you do to become more of a "big picture" kind of person?

## THEN WHAT?

In light of this passage, what personal commitment can you make?

**XTRA READING**
PHILIPPIANS 1

#ONTRACKDEVOS

## PHILIPPIANS 2:1-11

**NOTHING**

### SAY WHAT?

Observation: What do I see?

### SO WHAT?

Interpretation: What does it mean?

### NOW WHAT?

Application: How does it apply to me?

### THEN WHAT?

Implementation: What do I do?

Isn't it convicting when God places specific words in a verse that make it impossible to justify our behavior or attitudes? Today's passage has one of those words. It is the word "nothing" found in verse 3. Paul tells us in today's reading that we are to do nothing out of selfish ambition or vain conceit. That leaves no room for any shades of gray or excuses. We are never to do anything out of a selfish desire to make ourselves look good. Our motives to serve in a position of leadership should never be for attention or personal recognition. We should never conduct ourselves in a way that could manipulate opinions. We should never do something to make people feel obligated to us. Instead, we are to always consider others better than ourselves. We are to think about what is best for them. Our motives for everything we do should be based on what is best for others. We, as Christians, have a high standard to live up to. We must never do anything out of selfishness, but always be motivated to help others. How do you measure up to what God expects? Are others a priority in your life? What specific area of your life has God spoken to you about today?

**XTRA READING**
PHILIPPIANS 2

## MOTIVATION

Why do you do "spiritual" things? Why do you go to church? Why do you have regular devotions? Why are you involved in a ministry at church? The answer to those questions is very important. It would be a pity to do the right things for the wrong reasons and not gain what God intended. In today's reading, we learn how the Apostle Paul came to realize that his own motivations were wrong at one time. He was doing good things, but he was doing them in order to gain favor with God, not out of love for God. He had to look closely at every area of his life and evaluate his motives for what he was doing. When he did, he found that he was trying to gain favor with God and make Him happy. That all changed. Suddenly, his motivation to gain favor with God was changed into KNOWING God. He wanted to have an intimate relationship with God. God had become real to him, and now he just wanted to know Him even better. What is your motivation for what you do? Do you open your Bible because you love Him and want to know Him more? Ask God to help you change the areas He has revealed. Besides, if you're His child, you already have His favor!

### SAY WHAT?

What motivation might someone have for doing spiritual things?

### SO WHAT?

How can you tell what your motivation for spiritual behavior is?

### NOW WHAT?

How can you tell if your motivation is simply to know Christ better?

### THEN WHAT?

In light of this passage, what personal commitment can you make?

**XTRA READING**

PHILIPPIANS 3

## PHILIPPIANS 3:12-21

### SAY WHAT?

Observation: What do I see?

### SO WHAT?

Interpretation: What does it mean?

### NOW WHAT?

Application: How does it apply to me?

### THEN WHAT?

Implementation: What do I do?

What words would you use to describe your spiritual life? Take some time to write down a few. As you look at those words, do they indicate that you are satisfied with where you are spiritually? If anyone could be satisfied with his spiritual level, it would be the Apostle Paul. But, look at what he says in today's reading. In verses 12 and 13, he says he has not yet obtained all he should in his walk with God. So, he continues to press on. He was not satisfied with his knowledge of Scripture, so he studied more. He was not content with the victory he had over sin in his life, so he worked even harder. He had spoken the message of Christ bodly and many were saved, but he wanted to become even better at soul winning. He forgot what was behind and pressed on to greater growth. He was devoted to winning the prize for which Christ had called him heavenward. Are you pressing on in your walk with God? Are you reading more than you did last year? Are you becoming better at overcoming sin? Make it your passion to work every day to be better than you were yesterday. Never be satisfied.

**XTRA READING**
PHILIPPIANS 3

## SUCH THINGS

We find in this passage one of the greatest verses in the Bible on how to control our minds. We are told to only think about things that are true, noble, right, pure, lovely, admirable, excellent, or praiseworthy. Since our minds control our behavior, we must be certain that only right thoughts are permitted to remain. Use the definitions provided today to evaluate what thoughts you allow in your mind. If any of your thoughts do not qualify, they are wrong and should not be allowed to remain. If you see problem areas, build a strategy to change. If you need help, ask. Make sure you are only thinking about the right things.

### SAY WHAT?

Observation: What do I see?

### SO WHAT?

Interpretation: What does it mean?

### NOW WHAT?

Application: How does it apply to me?

### THEN WHAT?

Implementation: What do I do?

**XTRA READING**

PHILIPPIANS 4

**IS AND DONE**

## SAY WHAT?
Who does this passage tell me Jesus Christ is?

## SO WHAT?
What does this passage tell me Jesus Christ did?

## NOW WHAT?
What should my response be to what I have written above?

## THEN WHAT?
In light of this passage, what personal commitment can you make?

If a friend from school or work were to ask you who Jesus Christ is, how would you answer him? What Scripture would you refer to that explains who He is? You could turn to this chapter to answer his question. Paul gives us some incredible details about Jesus' identity. Not only does this passage tell us who Jesus Christ is, it also reveals to us what He has done. For example, vs. 21 tells us that once we were alienated from God and enemies in our minds but, through the death of Jesus Christ, we were reconciled to God. Jesus came to this earth and took on the form of a man. He lived a perfect life and paid the debt of sin through His death on the cross. We can have peace with God because of the blood He shed on the cross. Why not take some time today to reflect on who Jesus is and what He has done for you. In fact, use today's questions to help you. You might even want to share it with others. This Scripture is too important to just keep to ourselves. Share it so others can know how they can trust Christ.

**XTRA READING**
COLOSSIANS 1

## ALL HIS ENERGY

What is the most important thing in your life? What consumes most of your time and thoughts? How do you spend your money? What do you always look to buy? Hopefully, it is the same thing that Paul described in today's reading. Paul was motivated by what Christ had done in his life and he wanted everyone, everywhere, to know this amazing truth. All his thoughts and energies were consumed by letting others know what Christ had done for him. His relationship with Christ was so amazing that he simply could not keep quiet. If having others come to know Christ meant labor and hard work on his part, then he was willing. All his energy was devoted to letting people know that Jesus Christ was the answer in their lives. Do you have this kind of commitment to see that others know what Jesus Christ has done in your life and can do in theirs? Is all your effort and energy devoted to this important task? Or is your energy devoted to academics, sports, work, relationships, possessions, or other worthless pursuits? In light of what Christ has given you, how can you not make sharing Him your #1 ambition? Examine your life and see what needs to change.

### SAY WHAT?
Observation: What do I see?

### SO WHAT?
Interpretation: What does it mean?

### NOW WHAT?
Application: How does it apply to me?

### THEN WHAT?
Implementation: What do I do?

**XTRA READING**

COLOSSIANS 1

## COLOSSIANS 2:16-23

## CHRIST ALONE

### SAY WHAT?
Observation: What do I see?

### SO WHAT?
Interpretation: What does it mean?

### NOW WHAT?
Application: How does it apply to me?

### THEN WHAT?
Implementation: What do I do?

What error was being taught in this church that Paul was so afraid people would follow? Why would those errors be so damaging? While Paul did not name them directly, we can see from his warnings that they fell into three categories; legalism, mysticism, and asceticism. Legalism attacks the sufficiency of Christ by saying you not only need Christ, but you must also follow other rules and regulations. Paul says, in verses 9-12, that Christ paid the price for us. Mysticism attacks Christianity by teaching that you not only need Christ, but you also need a deeper, higher, religious experience. Paul explained, in verses 16-19, that the people who teach this have lost connection with the Head. Christ has given us all we need. Asceticism attacks Christ by teaching that we not only need Christ, but we also need to live a life of self-denial. It teaches that we must live in poverty. Paul, however, says in verses 20-23, that while this may look spiritual, living this way has no power over sin. Your salvation has given you all you need. You need nothing else but Christ and His Word! Have any of these errors affected your understanding? How can you change it?

XTRA READING
COLOSSIANS 2

## LET

This chapter teaches us how to put into practice what we learned yesterday in Colossians 2. Paul tells us that since human standards and regulations do not give us any power over sexual sin, we are to set our hearts and minds on things above. What motivates us and occupies our thoughts ought to be eternal. How do we do this? He explains in this chapter the process we must go through. Let's focus on the last three. In verse 15, he tells us we accomplish this by letting the peace of Christ RULE in our hearts. The word means to umpire or govern over. In verse 16, we are told to do this by letting the Word of Christ, which is the Bible, DWELL in us. That word means to inhabit, abide, or remain in. Finally, we are told in verse 17, that we do this by DOING everything in the name of God. That means we are always aware of our dependence on God--that we live under God's authority, and that we are His representatives in this world. Are you doing these three? Use today's questions to create ways to begin changing. Remember, it is not through rules, a religious experience, or self denial that we gain spiritual maturity. It is through Christ and His Word.

### SAY WHAT?

In what ways can you begin to allow the peace of Christ to rule in my heart?

### SO WHAT?

In what ways can you begin to allow the Word of God to dwell in me richly?

### NOW WHAT?

In what ways can you begin to do everything in the name of God?

### THEN WHAT?

What personal commitment can you make in light of what this passage teaches?

### XTRA READING

COLOSSIANS 3

## COLOSSIANS 4:1-6

## EVERY OPPORTUNITY

### SAY WHAT?
Observation: What do I see?

### SO WHAT?
Interpretation: What does it mean?

### NOW WHAT?
Application: How does it apply to me?

### THEN WHAT?
Implementation: What do I do?

How many opportunities in a typical day do you have to impact others? How many opportunities did you have yesterday to give a word of encouragement to someone who was really discouraged and ready to give up? How many opportunities will you have today to plant a seed that will help someone make an important decision in his future? How many opportunities will you have tomorrow to share something about your faith that will encourage an unsaved friend to think about his relationship with Christ? How many opportunities will you have to demonstrate to someone who is watching the difference that Jesus Christ makes in your life? If you are honest, you would have to answer all of those questions with the word "many." With that knowledge in mind, Paul closed this letter with an important admonition. He told them to make the most of "every" opportunity. What a great prayer for you each day. "Today, God help me to see the opportunities to impact others and make the most of every one You send my way." Why not start each day with this simple prayer and watch what God does in your life!

### XTRA READING
COLOSSIANS 4

# WILDERNESS OUTFITTING

The longest-standing tool in our toolbox, the **Wilderness Outfitting** program presents an opportunity for the intentional leader to gain abnormal access to **real connection** with those they lead.

The wilderenss can be leveraged into significant access to **real relationships** and **real conversations** that defy other environments... and it transfers back home beautifully.

Photos by **Katie Hall** from a 2016 Pilgrimage trip with Ogletown Baptist Church (DE).
**katiehallcreative.com**

THEREFORE, SINCE WE ARE SURROUNDED BY SO GREAT A CLOUD OF WITNESSES, LET US ALSO LAY ASIDE EVERY WEIGHT, AND SIN WHICH CLINGS SO CLOSELY, AND LET US RUN WITH ENDURANCE THE RACE THAT IS SET BEFORE US...
HEBREWS 12:1 (ESV)

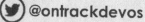

# ontrack devotions

## MARCH
### 2017
HEBREWS
JAMES

# MONTHLY PRAYER SHEET

"...The prayer of a righteous man is powerful and effective." James 5:16

| Reach out... | How I will do it... | How it went... |
| --- | --- | --- |
| | | |

| Other requests... | Answered | How it was answered... |
| --- | --- | --- |
| | | |

**Name:** _____

This sheet is designed to help you make personal commitments each month that will help you grow in your walk with God. Fill it out by determining
1. What will push you
2. What you think you can achieve

If you need help filling out your commitments, seek out someone you trust who can help you. Share your commitments with those who will help keep you accountable to your personal commitment.

### Personal Devotions:
How did I do with my commitment last month? _____
I will commit to read the OnTrack Bible passage and devotional thought _____ day(s) each week this month.

### Church Attendance:
How did I do last month with my attendance? _____
I will attend Youth/Growth Group _____ time(s) this month.
I will attend the Sunday AM service _____ time(s) this month.
I will attend the Sunday PM service _____ time(s) this month.
I will attend _____ time(s) this month.
I will attend _____ time(s) this month.

### Scripture Memory:
How did I do with Scripture memory last month? _____
I will memorize _____ key verse(s) from the daily OnTrack Devotions this month.

### Outreach:
How did I do last month with sharing Christ? _____
I will share Christ with _____ person/people this month.
I will serve my local church this month by _____
_____

### Other Activities:
List any other opportunities such as events, prayer group, etc., that you will participate in this month. _____
_____

## ANGELS

If someone at school or work asked you who Jesus Christ is, or what you thought about angels, what would you tell him? You could take him to today's reading. In it, we see that Jesus Christ is superior to every living thing. Specifically, He is superior to angels. Verses 1-3 teach us that Jesus Christ is God. He is the exact representation of God. The word translated "representation" here means that He is equal to God in every way. He radiates the glory of God because He is totally God in every way. He is, therefore, not like the angels. He is not a higher form of an angel. He is superior to angels in every way because He is totally God. The book of Hebrews further demonstrates this truth by showing us that the Father talks to Jesus in ways He has never spoken to angels. Also, we see that angels are not to be worshiped, but Jesus Christ is. Angels do not rule on thrones, but Jesus Christ does. Because He is fully God, Jesus Christ will never change or fail us. He alone, not angels, is to be worshiped and adored. Since angels or other spiritual beings can be a topic of conversation, why not use the opportunity to share Christ? Will you be ready?

### SAY WHAT?
Observation: What do I see?

### SO WHAT?
Interpretation: What does it mean?

### NOW WHAT?
Application: How does it apply to me?

### THEN WHAT?
Implementation: What do I do?

XTRA READING

HEBREWS 1

## HEBREWS 2:5-18

# A MAN

### SAY WHAT?

What temptations are you now facing?

### SO WHAT?

How are your temptations like those Jesus faced?

### NOW WHAT?

How did Jesus respond to His temptations?

### THEN WHAT?

Write out a prayer asking Jesus to help you be victorious over the temptations you are facing.

Why did Jesus Christ have to become a man? In today's reading, we are given some important reasons why Jesus had to come to earth as a man. One of those is found in verses 9 and 17. Jesus Christ became a man so that He could die on behalf of all of us. He paid the price for our sin so that we do not have to pay it ourselves. A second reason is given in verse 14. Jesus Christ became a man so that He might destroy Satan and his power over death in order to free us from the fear of death. A third reason is given in verses 17 and 18. This reason is so important for our daily living, but few seem to realize it is true. We are told that Jesus Christ became a man so that He might become a merciful and faithful High Priest. Because He willingly became a man, He knows the daily experiences of a man and responds to us out of His personal knowledge of what we face. Verse 18 tells us that He is able to help us when we are tempted because He has faced the same temptations. Jesus not only knows what we face today, but He is able to help each of us resist temptation. What temptation are you facing that you can take to Him for help?

**X**TRA READING
HEBREWS 2

## HARD HEARTS

**HEBREWS 3:7-19**

So far in our reading of the book of Hebrews, we have come across two strong warnings to pay careful attention to the moving of God in our lives. We are further warned that when He does move in our lives, we need to respond. In today's reading, we are given another warning. We are not to harden our hearts and miss salvation. God knows it is possible to grow up in a Christian environment and be able to recite the truth, and yet not have trusted Christ. God also knows it is possible to grow up around godly people and influences, and yet allow our hearts to become hardened toward God. How do we avoid a hardened heart? According to verses 7 and 8, we avoid it by responding to God's prompting. The author tells us that if we hear the voice of God today, we must respond immediately and not wait until another time. We must not excuse or justify a delay. When God convicts our hearts, we must not wait to respond. If we don't act upon the conviction God brings, we are heading for hardened hearts. Has God convicted you of an area that you have not yet responded to? Right now would be a good time to start!

### SAY WHAT?
Observation: What do I see?

### SO WHAT?
Interpretation: What does it mean?

### NOW WHAT?
Application: How does it apply to me?

### THEN WHAT?
Implementation: What do I do?

**X**TRA READING
HEBREWS 3

**o d**

## HEBREWS 4:8-13

### SAY WHAT?

How would you describe the time you spend in God's Word?

### SO WHAT?

In what ways has God used His Word recently in your life?

### NOW WHAT?

What needs to change in your life so that God's Word is able to be living and active in your heart?

### THEN WHAT?

In light of this passage, what personal commitment can you make?

What words would you use to describe the Bible? Write down what you came up with in the margin of your OnTrack. What words did you use? Did you choose the same words the Holy Spirit used in this passage of Scripture--living and active? Why did He choose these two specific words? He did so because He wanted us to understand that the Bible is unlike any other book. It is not stagnant or just words on a page. It is alive and can penetrate even to our souls. God's Word is what judges our hearts and reveals to us areas that need work. God's Word is what judges our thoughts and attitudes to make sure they are in line with what God desires. Everything is laid bare before God and His Word when we read it. We must be diligent to read and study this Book so it can do its work in our hearts. It will change our lives as we read it. How much time do you spend in God's Word each day? Do you make the effort every day? Are you spending the kind of time that allows it to work in your heart? If we neglect our time in God's Word, we will lack the ability to accurately examine our lives or to receive guidance in our decision making. Neglecting Scripture is dangerous.

XTRA READING
HEBREWS 4

The book of Proverbs was designed to help us in "attaining wisdom and discipline; in understanding words of insight; in acquiring a disciplined and prudent life, doing what is right and just and fair; in giving prudence to the simple, knowledge and discretion to the young." As you read through this chapter, write down the verses that are most significant to you in your present circumstances.

| VERSE | WHAT TRUTH IT COMMUNICATES | HOW IT IMPACTS MY LIFE |

## HEBREWS 5:1-10                                    OUR PRIEST

### SAY WHAT?
Observation: What do I see?

### SO WHAT?
Interpretation: What does it mean?

### NOW WHAT?
Application: How does it apply to me?

### THEN WHAT?
Implementation: What do I do?

In these next few chapters of Hebrews, the author writes about Jesus being our High Priest. Why is it important for us to understand this truth? The answer is so that we can properly understand how to respond to God. In the Old Testament, people needed a mediator between God and themselves, someone who would go to God on their behalf. That person was the priest. Under the New Covenant, Jesus Christ became that person. We are now under the New Covenant and, therefore, do not need to go to a priest for forgiveness. We do not need to ask a priest to talk to God on our behalf. Jesus Christ is our High Priest and He does that for us. While there are other religions today who still believe one must go to God through a human priest, this section of Scripture makes it clear that this position is not Biblical. Jesus Christ was God, who became a man. He was our High Priest and offered Himself as our sacrifice. His sacrifice was all that was needed to provide us access to God. He now sits at the right hand of God, interceding for us. When we want to confess sin or need help, we go directly to Him. He is our High Priest. Are you going to Him like you should?

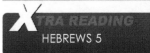

**XTRA READING**
HEBREWS 5

## SPIRITUAL BABIES                    HEBREWS 5:11-6:12

Have you ever tried to explain something to someone who should have been able to understand what you were saying, but he did not get it? Even though he had information that should enable him to understand, he still missed it. In this passage, the author of Hebrews faces this same challenge. He expresses, in verse 11, a desire to share more fully, but slowness of their learning prohibits him from doing so. Why? Because they had not been growing in their walks with God and were still spiritual babies. It was not because what he was sharing was difficult or complicated, as some might say, but because they had failed to grow in their knowledge of God's Word. By this point, they should have been teachers, but were still spiritual babies. Where are you in your walk with God? Does your pastor have to adjust what he says because you have not grown in your faith and in your knowledge of Scripture? How much have you grown spiritually since you trusted Christ? If you are still a baby and can't understand God's truths, what do you need to do in order to grow as God desires? Who can help you?

### SAY WHAT?

Why do so many Christians fail to grow in their walks with God?

### SO WHAT?

How can you begin to consistently grow in your walk with God?

### NOW WHAT?

How can you grow in your understanding of His Word?

### THEN WHAT?

In light of this passage, what personal commitment can you make?

XTRA READING
HEBREWS 5 AND 6

O⊕d

#ONTRACKDEVOS

## HEBREWS 7:11-28

### SAY WHAT?

Observation: What do I see?

### SO WHAT?

Interpretation: What does it mean?

### NOW WHAT?

Application: How does it apply to me?

### THEN WHAT?

Implementation: What do I do?

What does verse 12 of today's reading mean when it says that because of a new priesthood, the Law must change? A closer look reveals the answer. The word translated here "change" means to put one thing in the place of another. The point is that Christianity has been put in the place of Judaism. Jesus' priesthood was not "added" to the Old Testament line of Aaron; He "replaced" it. The "ceremonial" system of the Law was changed since Jesus Christ became the High Priest. God's "moral" law, however, did not change. God's standard of righteousness remained the same. While we no longer need to go to the Temple to offer sacrifices as under the ceremonial law, the definition of sin--the moral law--remains the same. In fact, under the new system of Christ, the moral law of God has been strengthened. It is now a higher standard of righteousness. We are now accountable for our attitudes and motivations, not just our actions. Jesus Christ has done what the Law could not. Jesus has taken the place of the old system. As a result, the standard is higher and we have direct access to God. We now can have full and complete forgiveness of sins.

XTRA READING
HEBREWS 7

## A RELATIONSHIP

What makes the New Covenant, (the New Testament system) superior to the Old Covenant, (the Old Testament system)? In this chapter, the author lists many reasons. The Old Covenant was basically established on external behavior. Obedience was usually a result of the fear of punishment. God's law was given on tablets of stone. The Holy Spirit, however, was not yet given to believers in the way the New Covenant allowed. After the Holy Spirit was given to the believers, the law of God was written on their hearts. True religion was no longer an external ritual, but an internal relationship. We see, in verse 11, that the New is better because it is personal. God lives within the hearts of all who by faith, have trusted Christ. We can have a personal relationship with God through Christ. In verse 12, the New Covenant is superior because it brings total forgiveness. The promise of the Old Testament was fulfilled. The Old Covenant only covered sin. Jesus Christ washed away our sin. How thankful are you for what He has done? Does your life demonstrate the difference between religion and relationship? It should!

### SAY WHAT?

What is the difference between external religion and an internal relationship?

### SO WHAT?

How can you tell if someone's life is based on external religion or an internal faith?

### NOW WHAT?

How can you prevent your life from becoming only external, like the old covenant?

### THEN WHAT?

In light of this passage, what personal commitment can you make?

XTRA READING

HEBREWS 8

## HEBREWS 9:6-14

### SAY WHAT?

Observation: What do I see?

### SO WHAT?

Interpretation: What does it mean?

### NOW WHAT?

Application: How does it apply to me?

### THEN WHAT?

Implementation: What do I do?

Is it possible to have a clear conscience even if you have committed horrible sins? Yes, if we understand what the New Covenant has done for us! This section is one of the greatest passages in the Bible for giving hope to our world. The author explains that the gifts and sacrifices under the Old Testament law were not able to "clear the conscience." Can you imagine that? Someone committed a sin, and even though it was covered by the blood of an animal, his conscience was not clean. Because we have a new system, our consciences can be clean. Verse 14 tells us that, because Jesus Christ shed His blood on the cross for us, and offered Himself unblemished to God, He can "cleanse" our conscience. We can have clean consciences because our sin is not just covered, but forgiven. If a guilty conscience is haunting you, Jesus Christ can wipe it clean--not just cover the sin. He can take it away and clear your conscience. People need to know what Jesus Christ has done for them and how they can be freed from the bondage of sin and the guilty conscience that follows. If you have experienced this cleansing yourself, why don't you be the one to tell them? A clean conscience is a gift from God.

### XTRA READING
HEBREWS 9

## FORGIVENESS

Today we learn what may be the most sought after commodity of mankind, and is available to all. What is it? Forgiveness!! Today's reading tells us how we can truly be forgiven. It is true that we have all sinned and fallen short of God's standard. Some may feel that they have violated God to a greater degree than others, and that may be true. However, the opportunity for forgiveness is not based on the seriousness of the offense, but on the ability to forgive on the part of the one who has been violated. We learn that Jesus Christ paid the price for our sin and made it possible, by His death on the cross, for us to obtain forgiveness. According to verse 17, not only can we obtain forgiveness, but God remembers our sin no more. Verse 18 tells us that where there has been forgiveness, there is no longer a need to sacrifice for sin. There isn't anything else we need to do to take care of it. We can live completely free from guilt. We are forgiven and everything is made new. Are you living as one who is forgiven? Can others see it in the way you act? As forgiven people, our lives should draw others to want it for themselves.

### SAY WHAT?

How can today's reading help those who still suffer from guilt over past sin?

### SO WHAT?

How can this passage help unsaved people who feel that their lives are too wicked to be forgiven?

### NOW WHAT?

How can today's reading help you with your feelings of guilt?

### THEN WHAT?

In light of this passage, what personal commitment can you make?

**XTRA READING**

HEBREWS 10

Ocd

## PROVERBS 30

The book of Proverbs was designed to help us in "attaining wisdom and discipline; in understanding words of insight; in acquiring a disciplined and prudent life, doing what is right and just and fair; in giving prudence to the simple, knowledge and discretion to the young." As you read through this chapter, write down the verses that are most significant to you in your present circumstances.

VERSE | WHAT TRUTH IT COMMUNICATES | HOW IT IMPACTS MY LIFE

## LET US

How did you respond to the kind of truth we read on Saturday? Is it simply something you log in your memory bank? Or is there some kind of action we should be taking? The passage of Scripture that we read today answers that question. There are five challenges to us all beginning with the words "let us." Number and circle them in your Bible. First, we are to draw near to God. We do that by faithfully reading His Word every day and spending time with Him in prayer. Second, we are to hold unswervingly to the hope we have. God is faithful--we should not doubt Him or lose our confidence. Third, we are to consider how we can spur one another on toward love and good deeds. That is, what can we do to challenge others to become more like Christ? Notice he used the word "spur." It may not be comfortable. Fourth, we need to make church attendance a priority. There isn't an option of whether or not to meet together. Finally, we are to encourage each other. We need to pray for others and ask how we can encourage them. How are you doing in these five areas?

### SAY WHAT?
In what ways do you struggle with these five?

### SO WHAT?
Why do you struggle in those areas?

### NOW WHAT?
In light of being forgiven, what can you do to better fulfill them?

### THEN WHAT?
In light of this passage, what personal commitment can you make?

**XTRA READING**
HEBREWS 10

# HEBREWS 11:1-16

## BY FAITH

### SAY WHAT?
Observation: What do I see?

### SO WHAT?
Interpretation: What does it mean?

### NOW WHAT?
Application: How does it apply to me?

### THEN WHAT?
Implementation: What do I do?

How could Abraham do what he did in today's reading? How could he leave his home, family and career with an uncertain destination and future? Because he had faith! He was sure that God would reward those who seek Him. He was certain that God existed. Therefore, Abraham knew he could trust God in what He was asking him to do. Today, it seems that many Christians want to know how everything is going to turn out before we step out for God. We may be willing to serve God, but we want to make sure we have something to fall back on in case it doesn't work out like we hope. We would take a stand for Christ if we knew what the outcome would be. For example, we don't want our children to get behind on homework due to church activities for fear it may hurt their GPA. We are in desperate need of students today who have a totally committed faith. We need students who are certain that God is real, and sure He will reward them for serving Him. This world needs to see adults and students alike who will move out for Him without concern or fear. Are you a teen with that kind of faith? Are you an adult who is encouraging teens to be bold? What is keeping you from being like those in this chapter?

### XTRA READING
HEBREWS 11

## THE UNNAMED

**HEBREWS 11:32-40**

Of all the men and women of faith listed in this chapter, which one leaves the greatest impact on you? As you read the list, did you identify with any one of them? While the list of those named is amazing, there were others whose names weren't specifically mentioned, who also did great things by faith. In fact, verses 33-38 list the great things they did. How incredible it must have been to be able to accomplish what these people did for God. How amazing to be able to stand for Christ against all odds. Verse 38 is accurate to say that the world was not worthy of them. Could your name ever be included in a chapter like this? Is it possible for us to have the kind of faith that would allow us to stand like they did? The answer is yes. In the passage we will read tomorrow, we will learn what is necessary in order to become men and women of faith. While it may never be required of us to be stoned, sawn in two, or chained and put into prison for our faith, we can take steps towards greater faith and standing for Christ in our worlds. Are you up to the demands this kind of faith will have on you? Are you this committed to Christ?

### SAY WHAT?
Observation: What do I see?

### SO WHAT?
Interpretation: What does it mean?

### NOW WHAT?
Application: How does it apply to me?

### THEN WHAT?
Implementation: What do I do?

**XTRA READING**

HEBREWS 11

## HEBREWS 12:1-17

### SAY WHAT?

What are some examples in your life of "things that hinder" or of "sin" that needs to be thrown off?

### SO WHAT?

In what ways can you "fix your eyes on Jesus" more consistently?

### NOW WHAT?

How can you do a better job of "running with perseverance"?

### THEN WHAT?

In light of this passage, what personal commitment can you make?

Today we see what is required in order to become people of faith. Mark them in your Bible. Number one, we must "throw off." We do so in two important areas. The first area we must "throw off" is everything that hinders. Those are the things that are not sin, but slow us down, distract, and entangle us in our walk with God. Examples can be TV, relationships, music, hobbies, movies, the computer, etc. The second area we must "throw off" is any sin that is in our lives. We cannot tolerate any sin, large or small, and expect to become people of faith. Number two, we must "run with perseverance." We must realize this is a long race and run without slowing down, no matter what we may face. Number three, we need to focus on Jesus Christ. He needs to be our priority and the only one we seek to please. It is a comfort to know that while we seek to do these three things, God will also do His work to keep us on track. How? Through His loving discipline. Whenever we get off track, He will discipline us to get us back where we need to be. However, we must allow that discipline to train us and not resist it. Answer the following questions to help you get started becoming a person of faith.

### XTRA READING
HEBREWS 12

## CONSUMING FIRE

HEBREWS 12:18-29

What words would you use to describe God? If you stopped people on the street and asked them this question, what answers do you think you would get? Some view God as a grandpa, someone who loves us and would never hurt us or send us to hell. He sits up in His rocking chair, pats us on the head, and tells us how much He appreciates how hard we are working on being good. Then, when we stand before Him on that day, He will just overlook our sin. Today's reading, however, gives us a very different picture of God. The writer of Hebrews tells us that God is a consuming fire (vs29). In light of that, we must worship Him with reverence and awe. A consuming fire is a long way from a grandpa in the sky who will excuse us when we fail. While it is true that God loves us deeply, we must also keep in mind that God is to be feared. His holiness demands He punish sin and deal with the unrighteous. Those who die without faith in Christ will spend eternity in hell. We must recognize who God is, serve Him faithfully, and share the Gospel with those who don't know the truth about Him. It is our responsibility. Are you fulfilling it?

### SAY WHAT?
Observation: What do I see?

### SO WHAT?
Interpretation: What does it mean?

### NOW WHAT?
Application: How does it apply to me?

### THEN WHAT?
Implementation: What do I do?

**XTRA READING**
HEBREWS 12

## HEBREWS 13:1-6

## BE CONTENT

### SAY WHAT?

Observation: What do I see?

### SO WHAT?

Interpretation: What does it mean?

### NOW WHAT?

Application: How does it apply to me?

### THEN WHAT?

Implementation: What do I do?

What words would you use to describe your life? Would you say you are happy? Content? What would it take for you to be able to use those words? In verse 5, the writer of Hebrews makes a powerful statement. It should cause each of us to ask some serious questions of ourselves. We are told that we should be content with whatever we have. Why? Because God has said He will never leave us or forsake us. In other words, even if we have nothing by the world's definition, we should still be content because God is with us. Even though we are not as attractive or as popular as we want to be, God is with us. Even though we do not have the posessions we might want, God is with us. Even though we are not as talented as we might wish to be, God is with us. This fact alone ought to make us content no matter what we have or where we are. To be unhappy with who we are or what we have is a statement to God that He is not enough. It is wrong to believe that in order to be happy and content, we need something besides Him. What does your level of contentment communicate about how much you value God's presence in your life? Is He enough for you?

**XTRA READING**
HEBREWS 13

The book of Proverbs was designed to help us in "attaining wisdom and discipline; in understanding words of insight; in acquiring a disciplined and prudent life, doing what is right and just and fair; in giving prudence to the simple, knowledge and discretion to the young." As you read through this chapter, write down the verses that are most significant to you in your present circumstances.

VERSE | WHAT TRUTH IT COMMUNICATES | HOW IT IMPACTS MY LIFE

**JAMES 1:1-18**                                    **PURE JOY**

## SAY WHAT?

What trials have you faced in the past?

## SO WHAT?

How has God used them to help you mature?

## NOW WHAT?

How can you apply this passage of Scripture in your life and then use it to help others as well?

## THEN WHAT?

In light of this passage, what personal commitment can you make?

What is so great about perseverance? James tells us that we should rejoice when trials come because they produce perseverance in our lives. The obvious question, then, is what is it about perseverance that makes trials something we should rejoice over? A word study in the New Testament for perseverance reveals that it means steadfast endurance toward aggression. It is the ability to stay put and stand our ground when opposition or hard times occur. It is the strength needed to never give up and patiently wait for God to work. Why is this quality so important? Because without it, we cannot successfully live the Christian life. It is the quality that leads to maturity and to ultimately becoming someone who lacks nothing (vs4). Without perseverance, we will remain immature. Trials produce the quality we need so desperately in our lives--perseverance. Without trials, we cannot have perseverance, and without perseverance, we will remain spiritual babies. Therefore, we rejoice in trials because God is helping us develop what we need to live the Christian life. How are you responding to trials? As though you value what they can produce?

**XTRA READING**
JAMES 1

## TRUE RELIGION

If you were to make a list of three characteristics that demonstrate someone is truly saved, what three would you choose? You probably would not choose the three James did in this passage. We need to examine our lives to determine if these three are evident in our behavior. The first test is that a true believer keeps a tight rein on his tongue (vs26). James uses this test because, according to Christ, the mouth reveals the true condition of one's heart. Listen to yourself talk and you will know the true condition of your heart. The second characteristic or test of true salvation is that they look after orphans and widows (vs27). The object of your charity reveals your motivation. Do you reach out to popular people who can do something for you? Or do you reach out to the unlovely or unpopular who really have nothing to benefit you? Third, James says that true religion keeps itself from being polluted by the world (vs 27). What we allow to influence us reveals the level of our commitment. What are you most influenced by? Friends, culture, sports figures, musicians? How do you measure up to these three? What changes need to be made?

### SAY WHAT?
Observation: What do I see?

### SO WHAT?
Interpretation: What does it mean?

### NOW WHAT?
Application: How does it apply to me?

### THEN WHAT?
Implementation: What do I do?

XTRA READING
JAMES 1

## JAMES 2:1-13

### SAY WHAT?

How is favoritism demonstrated in your church, workplace, or school?

### SO WHAT?

How is favoritism demonstrated in your own life?

### NOW WHAT?

What should you do to stop showing favoritism and love others the way Christ loves them?

### THEN WHAT?

In light of this passage, what personal commitment can you make?

How would you define favoritism? Does it exist in your church or school? What can you do about it? The answers to these questions are found in today's reading. The word translated favoritism, in verse 1, means "to show partiality based on outward appearance." Favoritism is being influenced by external things like appearance, possessions, being admired, education, etc. The example James gives illustrates what it looks like. This church treated people differently, not based on what was in their hearts, but on what others saw outwardly. The rich man got kindness and a great seat, the poor man did not. That is sin and shows that they judged people and were evil in their thoughts. James then demonstrates that God does not show favoritism based on external conditions. In fact, the poor have a greater opportunity for spiritual growth than the rich. Do you show favoritism? Are there people in your world that you don't associate with or talk to because of external conditions like appearance, the school they attend, their job, or wealth? In what ways do you need to change? Use today's questions to help you get started.

**XTRA READING**
JAMES 2

## SAVING FAITH

James asks a very important question in verse 14. The question itself illustrates that it is possible to have a faith that will not save you. The answer is vitally important. James asks whether or not a person's faith, which is not accompanied by action, can save him. In other words, if someone says he is saved, but does not have actions that demonstrate it, is he really saved? As you read through this section, it becomes obvious that James' answer is no. This kind of faith does not save. Can a person who claims to be saved really be saved if he doesn't reach out and meet the needs of others when he becomes aware of them? Does just believing in your head and knowing factually that Jesus is God and that He died and rose again get you to heaven? According to James, no it isn't. Is he saying, then, that we are saved by our works? No! He uses Abraham and Rahab to illustrate that works do not save you. His point is that if you really have saving faith, you will demonstrate it by the way you live. Saving faith is manifested by the way you act. So, what do your actions tell you about your faith? Is it the kind of faith that saves?

**SAY WHAT?**

Observation: What do I see?

**SO WHAT?**

Interpretation: What does it mean?

**NOW WHAT?**

Application: How does it apply to me?

**THEN WHAT?**

Implementation: What do I do?

**X**TRA READING

JAMES 2

o⊕d

#ONTRACKDEVOS

## JAMES 3:1-12

### SAY WHAT?

Observation: What do I see?

### SO WHAT?

Interpretation: What does it mean?

### NOW WHAT?

Application: How does it apply to me?

### THEN WHAT?

Implementation: What do I do?

There are four important principles in today's reading to illustrate the need to gain control of our tongues. Highlight or number them in your Bible. The first one is found in verses 3-4. We see that although the tongue is small, it can do great damage. With a few small words, we can cause someone great pain. The second principle is found in verse 5. There, we learn that the tongue can do irreparable damage. We can say things that hurt people in a way that permanently damages our relationship and our ability to influence their lives positively. Third, we learn in verses 7-8 that if we are going to tame our tongues, we need the power of God. We cannot gain control of the tongue by using the human strength God has given us. Fourth, verses 9-12 tell us that the tongue has equal potential for good and evil. It can be used in great ways for God, or it can be a tool of Satan to do damage to the cause of Christ. So much damage in people's lives and in the life of the church is done with the tongue. How is your tongue being used? Have you allowed the Spirit of God to control your tongue so that everything you say pleases God? Commit to that today.

**XTRA READING**
JAMES 3

## TRUE WISDOM

What kind of wisdom are you using? Does your wisdom come from God or from this world? Is there a way for you to be able to tell which kind of wisdom you are using? You could use today's reading to help you find out. In this section, James defines two kinds of wisdom to help us avoid using the world's wisdom. First, he demonstrates the different motives between worldly wisdom and God's wisdom. The world's wisdom is motivated by envy and selfish ambition. God's wisdom is pure, peace-loving, considerate, and submissive (vs17). Second, these two kinds of wisdom also have different sources. Worldly wisdom's source is the depraved human mind, the world, and sometimes Satan himself. God's wisdom comes from God and His Word. He enables us to make wise choices and decisions. Third, James tells us that these two kinds of wisdom have different results. The world's wisdom results in disorder and every evil thing. God's wisdom results in a harvest of righteousness. If you want to know what wisdom you are living by, just examine your motives, your source, and the results you are getting. It will be obvious if you are honest.

### SAY WHAT?

How can you tell what your motives are when you make decisions?

### SO WHAT?

How do you decide what your source of wisdom really is?

### NOW WHAT?

What do the results of your decisions tell you about the type of wisdom you use?

### THEN WHAT?

In light of this passage, what personal commitment can you make?

**XTRA READING**

JAMES 3

## PROVERBS 1

The book of Proverbs was designed to help us in "attaining wisdom and discipline; in understanding words of insight; in acquiring a disciplined and prudent life, doing what is right and just and fair; in giving prudence to the simple, knowledge and discretion to the young." As you read through this chapter, write down the verses that are most significant to you in your present circumstances.

VERSE | WHAT TRUTH IT COMMUNICATES | HOW IT IMPACTS MY LIFE

## FRIENDSHIP

What does it mean to have friendship with the world? Does it mean that we should not be friends with unsaved people at work or school? James gives us this important principle, and we need to understand it so we do not violate it or apply it in error. First, the world James has in mind is not planet earth or the people on it. He is talking about the world's system or society. He is not saying we should not be friends with people in the world. He is warning us against being "friendly" with the world's views and positions. The world's philosophy says that money is number one. I am friends with the world when I believe that and make decisions based on it. The world says I should seek to be first and look out for #1. I am friends with the world when I make that my life's philosophy. We should never support or encourage this kind of philosophy. If we do, we stand in direct opposition to God. Friendship with the world's system is enmity or separation from God. How friendly are you with the world? Do you allow its values to affect your decisions now and for the future? Have you adopted its goals for your own life? Are there ways you are developing friendships with the world?

### SAY WHAT?
Observation: What do I see?

### SO WHAT?
Interpretation: What does it mean?

### NOW WHAT?
Application: How does it apply to me?

### THEN WHAT?
Implementation: What do I do?

XTRA READING
JAMES 4

 #ONTRACKDEVOS

## JAMES 4:13-17

### SAY WHAT?

Observation: What do I see?

### SO WHAT?

Interpretation: What does it mean?

### NOW WHAT?

Application: How does it apply to me?

### THEN WHAT?

Implementation: What do I do?

Do verses 13-17 mean that we should not plan for the future? There are some who teach these verses suggest that. A closer examination of this section reveals a very different perspective. James' point is that there are many people who make plans for their future without ever considering God and what He might have planned for them. They have decided what college to attend, where to work, what their summer plans are, or even made carrer goals all without ever considering what God would have them do. James is making the point here that we do not know what will happen tomorrow and we do not know how long our life will be, so how can we make plans without God--who knows both of those things? Instead of making our own plans, we should seek His direction for our lives. Verse 17 takes it even a step further. To make plans without considering God is not only a bad idea, it is sin. James tells us that the one who knows that he ought to seek God's direction and doesn't do it, sins. That is true with any decision you make. What plans are you considering? Have you sought God's direction? Why not ask Him about it right now? He knows the future and how long you have.

### XTRA READING

JAMES 4

## PATIENCE

Do you ever feel like giving up? You have tried your best to make it through, but nothing seems to be changing. There is no end in sight, and you just can't go on anymore. If you could just be sure that God was going to move, you could hold on a little longer, but you just can't. If that is how you feel right now, or if you know someone who feels like this, today's passage will bring comfort. James tells us to be patient. He reminds us that the Lord is coming and we need to keep holding on. His example is the farmer who plants his seed and then waits patiently for the crop to come. Rain comes and goes, sunshine comes and goes, and then the harvest arrives. James says likewise we need to stand firm and not give in to the trials we are facing. God's coming is near, and we must hold on. We must also remember the prophets who were before us. They set an example for us to follow. They faced great trials, but one day the end came. What are you now facing that makes you feel as though you can't go on? Be patient. God is at work, and He will always move on your behalf. Don't give up! God might just be ready to move!

### SAY WHAT?

Why is it sometimes so hard to keep on going?

### SO WHAT?

Who in Scripture faced trials similar to your current situation?

### NOW WHAT?

How can you use their examples as encouragement in your circumstances?

### THEN WHAT?

In light of this passage, what personal commitment can you make?

**XTRA READING**

JAMES 5

## JAMES 5:13-20

## POWERFUL AND EFFECTIVE

### SAY WHAT?

Observation: What do I see?

### SO WHAT?

Interpretation: What does it mean?

### NOW WHAT?

Application: How does it apply to me?

### THEN WHAT?

Implementation: What do I do?

Of all the examples available in Scripture, why did James use Elijah as the example of what a righteous man could do through prayer? The reason is exciting. James lets us know that the prayer of a righteous man is powerful and effective. Would those two words describe your prayer life? All we have to do is to be righteous, and we can have a prayer life that is powerful and effective. Elijah is the example James uses. In 1 Kings 18, he was a man who demonstrated what we would expect from a righteous man: boldness, courage, confidence, zeal, valiance, and empowerment by God. However, in chapter 19, we see that there were occasions when this righteous man was scared, discouraged, lonely, and blind to what God was doing in his life. He doubted God's plan--doubts we wouldn't normally associate with a righteous man. The point James is making is that He was a man "just like us." James wants us to know that we can be righteous people and have powerful and effective prayers like Elijah. Why? Because we are often just like him. Why not go to prayer right now, utilizing the great power of prayer, just like Elijah!

**XTRA READING**
JAMES 5

## SUMMARY JAMES 1:22-25

Take some time today to review your reading this past month, and reflect on what God has taught you or convicted you about. Use today's questions to help you consider how what you have read should or has impacted your life. Spend time praying and asking God to help you make the changes you have identified. Look forward to what God is going to do next month as you spend time in His Word.

### SAY WHAT?

What have you learned from this month's reading?

### SO WHAT?

What section in this month's reading had the greatest impact on you? Why?

### NOW WHAT?

How do you want to be different in light of this month's reading?

### THEN WHAT?

What do you need to do to see those changes become a reality?

**XTRA READING**
JAMES 1-5

O✝d

I SURRENDER
I SURRENDER ALL

# MOMENTUM
## YOUTH CONFERENCE
# 2017

### July 18 - 23, 2017
### Indiana Wesleyan University, Marion, IN

Everyone is in need of a comeback. No matter how far they've wandered or what they've done, God is a God of calling His people to Himself. Whether we are coming to Him for the first time in His redemptive grace for salvation or realizing that as His child we have a need to come back to Him every day, everybody needs a comeback.

Don't miss the #bestweekofsummer with nine incredible main sessions, fun time with your friends, staying on a college campus, impactful hands-on ministry and so much more!

CE NATIONAL

THE COME BACK
AN EXTRAORDINARY POWER FOR THE EVERYDAY FOLLOWER

## buildmomentum.org
## Register after February 1!

OnTrackDevotions.com

# COMING SOON
## RETURN OF THE KING

ontrack devotions

APRIL
2017
REVELATION

# MONTHLY PRAYER SHEET

**"...The prayer of a righteous man is powerful and effective." James 5:16**

| Reach out... | How I will do it... | How it went... |
| --- | --- | --- |
|  |  |  |

| Other requests... | Answered | How it was answered... |
| --- | --- | --- |
|  |  |  |

**Name:** _____

This sheet is designed to help you make personal commitments each month that will help you grow in your walk with God. Fill it out by determining
1. What will push you
2. What you think you can achieve

If you need help filling out your commitments, seek out someone you trust who can help you. Share your commitments with those who will help keep you accountable to your personal commitment.

**Personal Devotions:**
How did I do with my commitment last month? _____
I will commit to read the OnTrack Bible passage and devotional thought _____ day(s) each week this month.

**Church Attendance:**
How did I do last month with my attendance? _____
I will attend Youth/Growth Group _____ time(s) this month.
I will attend the Sunday AM service _____ time(s) this month.
I will attend the Sunday PM service _____ time(s) this month.
I will attend _____ time(s) this month.
I will attend _____ time(s) this month.

**Scripture Memory:**
How did I do with Scripture memory last month? _____
I will memorize _____ key verse(s) from the daily OnTrack Devotions this month.

**Outreach:**
How did I do last month with sharing Christ? _____
I will share Christ with _____ person/people this month.
I will serve my local church this month by _____
_____

**Other Activities:**
List any other opportunities such as events, prayer group, etc., that you will participate in this month. _____
_____

## SOON

Today you begin a journey that might be brand new for you, but one that you can be excited about. Today, you begin your journey through the book of Revelation. It is a book that everyone seems to be interested in, but a book that few have read through completely. As you begin, keep in mind some important points John gives to us as he begins this book. The first is that this book is the revelation of Jesus Christ, which God gave to John. It is not John's opinions or his own personal perceptions about the future. What you will be reading came directly to John from God. He simply wrote down what he saw (vs11). Second, it is important to know the reason God gave John this book. God wanted us to be able to know what will soon take place (vs1). This book is our glimpse of what is coming in the future. Third, it comes with a promise from God. John tells us that we will be blessed if we read it, hear it, and take to heart what it says. Although you may not catch everything your first time through, you will learn much that will excite and challenge you. Be faithful to your daily reading. Also, be faithful to apply to your life what you have read. Use today's questions to help you get started.

### SAY WHAT?

What do you hope to gain from reading this book?

### SO WHAT?

What do you hope to learn?

### NOW WHAT?

What will you need to do to see these two goals take place?

### THEN WHAT?

In light of this passage, what personal commitment can you make?

XTRA READING

REVELATION 1

## PROVERBS 2

The book of Proverbs was designed to help us in "attaining wisdom and discipline; in understanding words of insight; in acquiring a disciplined and prudent life, doing what is right and just and fair; in giving prudence to the simple, knowledge and discretion to the young." As you read through this chapter, write down the verses that are most significant to you in your present circumstances.

VERSE  |  WHAT TRUTH IT COMMUNICATES  |  HOW IT IMPACTS MY LIFE

## FIRST LOVE

Over the next seven days, we will be reading God's personal message to the seven churches. These were actual local bodies of believers at the time this book was written. In most cases, the letters contain positive characteristics followed by God revealing what was wrong with each of the churches. Today, we read about the church in Ephesus. This was a church that had much to be proud of. A positive characteristic God gave to these believers was that they had persevered in the midst of hardship. It was not a church that had given in when the pressure was on. It was also a church that did not tolerate wickedness. However, it was a church whose people had lost their first love. The joy and excitement they once had about their faith was gone. The fire that once burned bright was out, and they were just going through the motions. God called them to remember where they once had been, repent, and come back to the place they previously held. Could this be true of you or your church? Have you or your church lost the fire and passion you once had? If so, remember, repent, and do the things you once did. Losing your first love is serious to God.

### SAY WHAT?

Observation: What do I see?

### SO WHAT?

Interpretation: What does it mean?

### NOW WHAT?

Application: How does it apply to me?

### THEN WHAT?

Implementation: What do I do?

XTRA READING
REVELATION 2

#ONTRACKDEVOS

## REVELATION 2:8-11

### SAY WHAT?

What opposition do you face or could you be facing these next few months?

### SO WHAT?

What could God desire to accomplish in your life through it?

### NOW WHAT?

How can today's reading help you be faithful in the midst of opposition?

### THEN WHAT?

In light of this passage, what personal commitment can you make?

Imagine that someone came to you at school or work and told you that when you left the building, some students were going to beat you up because of the stand you had taken for Christ. What thoughts would run through your mind? That is exactly what happened to this church. The church in Smyrna had two characteristics they were known for. They were afflicted and poor. Yet, in spite of that, God said they were rich. They did not allow their afflictions or their poverty to cause bitterness or discouragement. God told them not to be afraid of what was ahead. God informed them that Satan would attack them. He would put some of the believers in prison and they would suffer for ten days. Their challenge? To remain faithful to God and He would give them the crown of life. It would have been comforting for those Christians to know that God was watching and knew exactly what was going on in their lives. He would help and reward them for their faithfulness. Are you experiencing any opposition in your life in which you need this encouragement? Underline verse 10 to remind you to remain faithful. Your reward is waiting for you!

### XTRA READING
REVELATION 2

## DOCTRINAL PURITY

How important is it to keep wrong doctrines and wrong teachings out of the local church? According to today's reading, it's crucial. God tells the church in Pergamum that there are some areas He is pleased with. The letter states that He knows that they have remained true to Him. Even when one of their leaders was put to death, they did not renounce their faith, but stayed true to what they believed. There is, however, something about this church He did not approve of. In spite of all the positive things about them, they had people in their church who held to teachings that were contradictory to God's law. One group specifically mentioned was the Nicolaitans. They taught that a Christian has liberty to do whatever he wants, even sexually, once he is saved. Although these believers had not yet denounced Christ in the midst of suffering, purity of doctrine was not a priority. God warned them that if they allowed this teaching to continue, it could cause others to fall into great sin. We often think that doctrine is not something we should be concerned about--each person can believe what he wants. God tells us that position is not true. Are you committed to doctrinal purity?

### SAY WHAT?

What doctrinal issues are you aware of that people in other churches disagree with?

### SO WHAT?

What could wrong views in those areas lead to?

### NOW WHAT?

How can you keep yourself from doctrinal error?

### THEN WHAT?

In light of this passage, what personal commitment can you make?

XTRA READING

REVELATION 2

## SAY WHAT?
Observation: What do I see?

## SO WHAT?
Interpretation: What does it mean?

## NOW WHAT?
Application: How does it apply to me?

## THEN WHAT?
Implementation: What do I do?

When John referred to a woman named Jezebel in this passage, was he referring to an actual woman in the church at Thyatira? Possibly, but that name most likely referred to a specific woman whose actions resembled those of Jezebel in the Old Testament. God saw this church and knew they had some good things going for them. They had a church of love and faith that resulted in service to others and perseverance in suffering. God told them that in the areas of service and perseverance, they had grown and increased. However, as in the case of the church of Pergamum, they tolerated a woman who led believers into committing sexual immorality and eating meat sacrificed to idols. Some believe that she may have even taught that homosexuality was permissible or that engaging in sex before marriage was fine if the couple loved each other. Whatever she taught, it led people into committing sin. We must never permit teaching that contradicts what the Bible says, or is not found in Scripture. If you can't defend it with Scripture, forget it.

**X**TRA READING
REVELATION 2

## DEAD

Can you imagine being in the church at Sardis when this letter was read? Everyone gathered together after having been told that a letter had arrived from God. The church sat quietly, waiting to hear what God had to say about what was right and what was wrong with them. God began by reminding them He knew their deeds and was aware of their reputation for being spiritually alive. When people evaluated this church, it appeared obvious that God was at work and it was filled with spiritual life and power. The obvious conclusion would seem to be that God was pleased and proud. But the reality was "I know you are dead." Although their reputation was that they were alive, they weren't. They fooled even themselves. His challenge--"wake up!" God warned that what life remained in the church was about to die. Think about how true this is for us. Could God say this about your life or your church? Do people think you are alive, but inside you know you are dead? As you take an honest look at your own life and your church, what do you see? Use today's questions to help you evaluate yourself and create a plan to respond to what you see.

### SAY WHAT?

What signs of spiritual life and power do you see in your life and your church?

### SO WHAT?

What signs indicate that you or your church could be close to dying?

### NOW WHAT?

What needs to happen in order to change it?

### THEN WHAT?

In light of this passage, what personal commitment can you make?

REVELATION 3

## REVELATION 3:7-13

### SAY WHAT?

Observation: What do I see?

### SO WHAT?

Interpretation: What does it mean?

### NOW WHAT?

Application: How does it apply to me?

### THEN WHAT?

Implementation: What do I do?

What is the difference between this and the other letters we have read so far? Look at it again and see if you notice the difference. It is that God did not give a single negative statement about this church. They were surely astonished to hear God approved of what they were doing and had no criticisms of them. He said He had given them an open door that no one would be able to shut. Although they had little strength, they still kept His Word and stayed true to His Name. It must have thrilled them to hear God say that those who opposed and criticized the church would one day publicly admit that God did love them. They had not only endured, but they had done so patiently. God's response was to keep them from the hour of trial—to take them away so they wouldn't have to face it. How would God evaluate you and your church? This passage should encourage us to see that it is possible to have a church about which God only makes positive statements. Could He describe your church this same way? Could He describe your life like this? What changes can you make in order for this to be said of you? What role can you play to begin the process?

### XTRA READING

REVELATION 3

The book of Proverbs was designed to help us in "attaining wisdom and discipline; in understanding words of insight; in acquiring a disciplined and prudent life, doing what is right and just and fair; in giving prudence to the simple, knowledge and discretion to the young." As you read through this chapter, write down the verses that are most significant to you in your present circumstances.

VERSE | WHAT TRUTH IT COMMUNICATES | HOW IT IMPACTS MY LIFE

## REVELATION 3:14-22

### SAY WHAT?

How would you rate your spiritual life as it is today on a scale of 0-10? Why that number?

### SO WHAT?

How does God feel about where you are in your walk with Him?

### NOW WHAT?

What needs to change in order for you to move to a higher number?

### THEN WHAT?

In light of this passage, what personal commitment can you make?

How would you rate your spiritual life? How do you think God feels about it? If we consider God's opinion, most of us should be concerned because our spiritual lives are only average. Many people evaluate their spiritual lives, and although they are not where they should be, they convince themselves that God is pleased they are not on the lowest levels of spiritual immaturity. That is not how God responds, however. In this letter to the Laodiceans, God says that lukewarm or average is worse than cold. How do you think the Laodiceans felt when they realized what God's position on average is? Why is it so wrong? Because it leads to wrong conclusions about the true condition of one's heart. The "average" Christian is convinced that he is okay. In fact, he thinks he is rich and needs nothing. In reality, he is wretched, pitiful, poor, blind, and naked. God's counsel is for him to repent of his sin and come back to Him. What is God's opinion of where you currently are in your walk with Him? What can you do about it?

XTRA READING
REVELATION 3

## WORTHY

Why is the message the four creatures gave different from what the twenty-four elders said to Christ? Could it be that the four creatures viewed God differently than the elders? The creatures, who had not experienced redemption, saw the holiness of God. In fact, all creation can recognize God's purity, His majesty, and His holiness. But to those of us who have been redeemed, He is more than just holy, He is worthy. Their song does not have the joy that the song of the redeemed has. The elders had once been dead in their sins and were slaves to sin. They had no ability to please God or know a way to be cleansed from sin. The provision for salvation through faith in Jesus Christ was revealed to them, and they accepted God's gift. When they stood before the throne of God, they laid down their crowns and said, "You are worthy." How someone responds to God reveals his view of God and the value he places on the gift God has given him. What does your response to God reveal about how you view Him? Does your life demonstrate you believe He is worthy? Why not take some time today to express to God how you feel about all He has done for you.

### SAY WHAT?
Observation: What do I see?

### SO WHAT?
Interpretation: What does it mean?

### NOW WHAT?
Application: How does it apply to me?

### THEN WHAT?
Implementation: What do I do?

XTRA READING

REVELATION 4

## REVELATION 5:1-10

### SAY WHAT?

Observation: What do I see?

### SO WHAT?

Interpretation: What does it mean?

### NOW WHAT?

Application: How does it apply to me?

### THEN WHAT?

Implementation: What do I do?

Who is the "Lion of the tribe of Judah‚Äù and the "Root of David?" How did He triumph? The answer to both of these questions is found by looking closely at this chapter. The Lion of the tribe of Judah and the Root of David was the One who was slain and, with His shed blood, purchased men for God. By His sacrifice, He made people of all nations to be a kingdom and priests of God. He was the Lamb who was slain. Who is the One who did all this? Jesus Christ. Because of what He did on the cross, He is worthy to not only open the scroll, but also to receive everything that belongs to God. He is worthy to receive power, wealth, strength, honor, glory, and praise. Jesus Christ did what no man could ever do. He did for you what you could never do for yourself. He purchased you for God, so that you might become a kingdom and a priest and serve Him. How have you responded to this truth? Hopefully, not only by worshiping and praising Him, but also by serving Him with your whole heart. After all He has done for us, is there a sacrifice too great or a task too menial to demonstrate our thankfulness and love? Is this how you live your life? It should be!

XTRA READING
REVELATION 5

In this chapter, we begin reading about how God is going to judge the world for its sinfulness. We, as Christians, will not be on the earth at this time because the Rapture will have taken us to heaven. Reading what takes place on earth at this time ought to motivate us to be more diligent in our witness. In this chapter, John reveals six of the seven seal judgments. They involve peace being removed from the earth and men beginning open war with each other. Famine covers the earth so severely that what once had been staples of life become luxuries. One-fourth of the population of the earth is killed by the sword, hunger, natural death, and wild beasts. There will also be major physical changes to the earth. The great earthquake will occur and the sun will be darkened like sackcloth. The moon will be reddened as blood and a meteor shower will pound the earth. Mountains and islands will be moved. It is hard to even imagine such devastation. What effect should these facts have on our lives? First, thankfulness towards God who saved us from this. Second, a renewed motivation to share Christ so that others will not have to experience these disasters.

## SAY WHAT?
Observation: What do I see?

## SO WHAT?
Interpretation: What does it mean?

## NOW WHAT?
Application: How does it apply to me?

## THEN WHAT?
Implementation: What do I do?

XTRA READING
REVELATION 6

#ONTRACKDEVOS

## REVELATION 7:9-17                                SALVATION

### SAY WHAT?

Write down the names of people you would love to see come to Christ.

### SO WHAT?

What obstacles could keep you from sharing Christ with them?

### NOW WHAT?

How will you go about sharing Christ with them in spite of those obstacles?

### THEN WHAT?

In light of this passage, what personal commitment can you make?

Why did God insert the account of the redemption of the 144,000 sealed Jews before describing the seventh seal? Maybe because it could be easy for one to assume, after reading about the seal judgments, that no one could get saved during such devastation. It is as if God stopped the account to let us know that in spite of what will occur on the earth, He will still save people. The activity of grace and men trusting in the Son of God for salvation will continue. John tells us that 144,000 Jews will be saved, as well as "a great multitude that no one could count." This group will be made up of all kinds of people. What a comfort to know that no matter how awful the circumstances may seem to us, or how wicked this world may get, God is still able to reach out and save people. In spite of what might be happening in their lives, there will be people who see their need to trust Christ. Who in your world needs to hear what Christ has done for them? Do not assume you know what their response will be or if their present environment will negatively affect their decisions. Do not allow assumptions to hinder sharing. Maybe, like today's reading, it is a time for grace!

### XTRA READING
REVELATION 7

## SILENCE

REVELATION 8:1-5

Why was there silence in heaven after the seventh seal was opened? As you read this chapter, you realize silence is about the only reaction one could have in response to what will be taking place. How would you respond to such news? Can you imagine what it is going to be like to live on the earth during the Tribulation? Think about this seventh seal judgment. One third of the earth will be burned up, a third of the sea will be turned to blood and, as a result, a third of the creatures in the sea will die. Can you imagine the smell that is going to create? Also, a third of the rivers become bitter and even more people will die. After the fourth trumpet sounds, a third of all the light from the sun and moon will be turned dark. A third of each day will be totally black. How horrible it will be for those left trying to survive the judgment of God during these days. Reading this ought to cause all of us to be more diligent in sharing the message of Christ with those who are headed for these judgments because they are not saved. Do you love your unsaved friends enough to share Christ with them? Who can you reach out to this week? What should you say to him?

### SAY WHAT?
Observation: What do I see?

### SO WHAT?
Interpretation: What does it mean?

### NOW WHAT?
Application: How does it apply to me?

### THEN WHAT?
Implementation: What do I do?

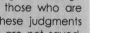

XTRA READING
REVELATION 8

## PROVERBS 4

The book of Proverbs was designed to help us in "attaining wisdom and discipline; in understanding words of insight; in acquiring a disciplined and prudent life, doing what is right and just and fair; in giving prudence to the simple, knowledge and discretion to the young." As you read through this chapter, write down the verses that are most significant to you in your present circumstances.

VERSE | WHAT TRUTH IT COMMUNICATES | HOW IT IMPACTS MY LIFE

## NO REPENTANCE

How would you respond if you were living on the earth during the Tribulation period? Can you even imagine experiencing what you have read in Revelation up to this point? God's judgment, however, is not finished. Today we read about even more of God's judgment. John reveals that there will be demonic forces coming up out of hell that will torture people for five months. People will be in such agony that they will want to die, but will not be able to. According to verse 6, death will elude them. Four angels will be released and they will kill a third of all mankind. Keep in mind that these two events follow the events found in chapter 8. One would assume that people would flock to God in repentance, seeking His mercy. One would think that, by now, they would be getting the message that God hates sin, and that they need to repent and seek His forgiveness. Do they? Not according to verse 20. They still do not stop worshiping demons and idols or repent. Sadly, we often do the same thing. God convicts us about sin in our lives, yet we refuse to repent. Could God be dealing with you right now about an area in which you need to repent and seek forgiveness?

### SAY WHAT?
Observation: What do I see?

### SO WHAT?
Interpretation: What does it mean?

### NOW WHAT?
Application: How does it apply to me?

### THEN WHAT?
Implementation: What do I do?

**XTRA READING**

REVELATION 9

## REVELATION 10:8-11

## EAT IT?

### SAY WHAT?

What are the most interesting things you have learned in Revelation so far this month?

### SO WHAT?

What are the most difficult things you have learned about the future?

### NOW WHAT?

What should your response be to what you are learning?

### THEN WHAT?

In light of this passage, what personal commitment should you make?

What is God trying to communicate to us from this interlude between the trumpet judgments? As He did before, John apparently stops his description of the judgments to encourage us. In this chapter, John saw a book that contained the events yet to come. John was told not to reveal them. He was then asked to do something that must have seemed bizarre. The voice of heaven told him to get the scroll and eat it. The angel said that it would taste sweet in his mouth, but then grow sour in his stomach. What reason could there be for doing that? Could God want us to know that His Word must get inside of us before we communicate it? Could He be illustrating the truth of this entire book? That prophecy compels us to read and study? The events of the future are exciting. However, when the reality of the future is comprehended, it sours in your stomach. This book, while exciting and interesting, ought to grieve the heart of every believer. What happened to John when he ate the scroll should happen to each of us as the Word really gets inside us. How have you responded to what you have read? What does your response tell you about yourself?

XTRA READING
REVELATION 10

## WITNESSES

With all that has gone on thus far in the Tribulation, one would think that the hearts of people would be softening. One would think that the survivors would be open to seeking God's forgiveness. However, in today's reading, we see that their hearts are, in fact, growing harder. We read that there will be two witnesses on the earth at this time. They will be a testimony to who God is and what He expects from them. The world will not respond well. For 1,260 days, the witnesses will preach, and no one will be able to harm them. After the appointed days are up, they will be killed. The people's mockery towards God is demonstrated by the desecration of the witnesses' bodies. The world will turn their deaths into a holiday of gift giving and celebration. What contempt! But God will intervene and will raise them from the dead and call them to heaven. A major earthquake will occur, and 7,000 more lives will be lost. God desires that we allow His judgment in our lives to soften us and bring us to repentance, not to harden our hearts against Him. Are there ways you are like these people in your response to God's judgment? Where does your heart need to be softened?

### SAY WHAT?
Observation: What do I see?

### SO WHAT?
Interpretation: What does it mean?

### NOW WHAT?
Application: How does it apply to me?

### THEN WHAT?
Implementation: What do I do?

**XTRA READING**
REVELATION 11

## REVELATION 12:1-12

### SAY WHAT?
Observation: What do I see?

### SO WHAT?
Interpretation: What does it mean?

### NOW WHAT?
Application: How does it apply to me?

### THEN WHAT?
Implementation: What do I do?

What does this chapter mean? Did you wonder what the answer to that question was as you read? Let's examine the passage closely and see if we can understand what John wrote. First, the woman in this chapter represents the nation of Israel. It is from them that Christ was born. The child is obviously Christ. The dragon is Satan. Satan tried, at the time of Christ's birth, to destroy Him, yet was unable to do so. Instead, Christ died for our sins and rose again the third day, accomplishing His purpose. Since Satan was unable to defeat the child, he turned his attention to the woman, the nation of Israel. In this chapter, we also learn that there will be a battle between Michael and God's army and Satan and his army. Satan will be defeated, probably in the middle of the Tribulation, and then cast out of heaven. He will not be permitted there again. Satan will intensify his attack on the nation of Israel. God will provide refuge so that they will not be totally defeated. This is the beginning of the end for Satan and his army. God will be victorious against Satan, and will provide deliverance for His people. Our ultimate victory is guaranteed no matter what it might look like today!

### XTRA READING
REVELATION 12

## PATIENCE AND ENDURANCE

Who is the first and second beast in this chapter? The first beast is commonly known as Antichrist. He is a man who will rule on the earth during the Tribulation and will be given his power and his throne by Satan himself. The second beast is known as the false prophet. His job will be to promote Antichrist and convince the world to worship him. Satan is attempting to counterfeit the trinity of God with these two evil beasts. He will set himself up as God and Antichrist as Jesus. Satan will even deceive people into believing that Antichrist has died of a head wound and is then raised back to life. All this is designed to counterfeit what God has done. It would seem hopeless if we did not know that God was in total control. While Satan may think he is in control, he is just accomplishing what God has designed. The saints are given great encouragement in verse 10 when they are told to have patient endurance and faithfulness. Likewise, when we face what may appear to be hopeless situations, we need faithfulness and endurance as we wait for God's solution. God is in control, even when it may look like He is not.

### SAY WHAT?

What circumstances are you facing that seem to be hopeless?

### SO WHAT?

What past situations have you faced that God delivered you from?

### NOW WHAT?

How can you find comfort in your present circumstances after reading this passage?

### THEN WHAT?

In light of this passage, what personal commitment can you make?

**XTRA READING**

REVELATION 13

OCD

## REVELATION 14:6-13             3 ANGELS

### SAY WHAT?
Observation: What do I see?

### SO WHAT?
Interpretation: What does it mean?

### NOW WHAT?
Application: How does it apply to me?

### THEN WHAT?
Implementation: What do I do?

The events that unfold in these last days seem to get more amazing with each passing chapter of Revelation. In this chapter, we read about the unique way that God will communicate the Gospel to people during the Tribulation. According to this chapter, God will send three angels who will fly around, calling out with a loud voice to people on earth. One will be calling for people to glorify God; one will proclaim that Babylon is fallen; and one will warn people not to worship the beast or get its mark. Why would God choose angels to communicate His message? In the midst of all the devastation that has gone on to this point, you would think that people would be ready to listen to an angel from heaven. But they won't, and will continue in their sin, refusing to humble themselves before God. The resulting judgment of God climaxes in the battle of Armageddon where the blood will be 4$f$|_ feet deep for 180 miles (vs 20). You should find comfort knowing that you do not have to be a part of this horror. Tragically, there are those who will reject God no matter the consequences. Why not pray for opportunities to help people avoid these coming horrors?

**XTRA READING**
REVELATION 14

## VICTORIOUS

Chapter 15 is an interlude before the most awesome of God's judgments against the world. In chapter 16, we will begin reading about the seven bowl judgments, which are even worse than what you have read so far. In the midst of learning about what will be taking place in heaven during this time, there is something important to keep in mind. Did you see it? It is found in verse 2. As John looked across the sea, he saw a group of people. Note how he described them. They were a group of people who were victorious over the beast. It could easily feel as if Satan will be victorious over everyone during the Tribulation. There still will be those, however, who will stand for God and be victorious over Satan. In fact, there will even be some who will still trust Christ as we read earlier. As we journey ahead in this book, and as the bowl judgments unfold, keep in mind that there will always be a group of people resisting Satan and standing for God. If that is true in the future, how much more ought we, in today's world, stand firm for Christ and live victorious. Are you one of those people?

### SAY WHAT?

Observation: What do I see?

### SO WHAT?

Interpretation: What does it mean?

### NOW WHAT?

Application: How does it apply to me?

### THEN WHAT?

Implementation: What do I do?

XTRA READING
REVELATION 15

## REVELATION 16:1-16

### SAY WHAT?

How does God reveal to you areas in which you need to repent?

### SO WHAT?

In what areas do you sense Him prompting you even now?

### NOW WHAT?

How can you avoid developing a hard heart that refuses to repent?

### THEN WHAT?

In light of this passage, what personal commitment can you make?

Why does God bring about these horrible judgments on the earth? We get part of the answer in today's reading. As we read through this chapter, we can't help but shudder at what it is going to be like to live on the earth during the bowl judgments. Imagine everyone having painful sores covering their bodies. Imagine the smell when every living thing in the sea dies, and the rivers and springs become blood. Imagine the agony and outcry when people are not just sunburned, but are scorched and seared. Why do all of these things happen? According to verse 6, it is because they have shed the blood of saints and prophets. They, even in the midst of all these judgments, have refused to humble themselves before God or even behave civilly to those who serve Him. Even verse 9 says that, in spite of their own physical pain from the sores and the sun, they refuse to repent or glorify God. These events end with an earthquake unlike any before it. Their response? Still no repentance. An unrepentant heart will lead to unbelievable hardness. Make sure this doesn't happen to you. It won't if you deal with your sin quickly and completely.

**X**TRA READING
REVELATION 16

## WORLD RELIGION

This is one of the chapters in Revelation that can be confusing to read. It helps if we understand some of the symbols given here. The beast, as we learned earlier, is Antichrist. The harlot is a symbol of the false religion that has been the world religion during the Tribulation. John explains that, in the beginning of the Tribulation, this false religion will flourish in the system of the world referred to as Babylon. It will center in Rome and will include other religious groups besides the Roman Catholic church. For the first half of the Tribulation, this religion will reign unchallenged; but in the middle of the Tribulation, Antichrist will destroy this religion and will set himself up as the one to be worshiped. John describes for us what the religion of the Tribulation will look like and how the world will follow it until it's destroyed by Antichrist. In spite of all that has gone on to this point, people will still refuse the true God and will worship the beast. They will simply adopt the new religion. While it may look bleak, God's victory is just around the corner. In fact, those of us in heaven are ready to go to war. Will that be you?

### SAY WHAT?
Observation: What do I see?

### SO WHAT?
Interpretation: What does it mean?

### NOW WHAT?
Application: How does it apply to me?

### THEN WHAT?
Implementation: What do I do?

**XTRA READING**
REVELATION 17

## REVELATION 18:9-18

## THE END

### SAY WHAT?

What circumstances do people face in this life that drain them of hope?

### SO WHAT?

Why is it so hard to trust God in circumstances like those listed above?

### NOW WHAT?

How can you use this passage to encourage others and yourself in difficult times?

### THEN WHAT?

In light of this passage, what personal commitment can you make?

Today you have read the final aspect of the judgment of God on the world. In it, we find some important and interesting truths. During the Tribulation, Babylon will not only become the center of religion in the world, but it will also become the commercial center of the world. Chapter 17 has revealed how the religion of Babylon will end. Chapter 18 reveals how the economic and commercial aspects of Babylon will end. In spite of all the death and devastation on the earth so far, those remaining will continue to have hope because of the wealth and power of Babylon. Read verses 11-13 to see the kind of luxury items that will still be available in this city. God will destroy it, however, and they will finally realize that it is all about to end. As they see the city burning, they will know that Babylon and its power and wealth has fallen under the mighty hand of God's judgment. Fear will grip the hearts of people when they realize the end is near. As believers, we are reminded again that although it may appear hopeless at the moment, appearances can be deceiving. God will always win. He's always victorious. Even in our lives today!

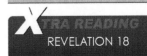

XTRA READING
REVELATION 18

## VICTORY

What a difference between this chapter and the other chapters we have been reading this month! Did you notice that as you read? Instead of gloom and doom, today we see the beginning of God's reign on the earth. As you read these events, remember that if you know Christ as your Savior, you will be participating in them. After the destruction of Babylon, Christ will come back to earth to set up His earthly kingdom. Heaven will begin its rejoicing, knowing that the time is almost here. Christ will mount His white horse and come to earth to destroy Satan and his armies. The beast and false prophet will be captured and cast into the Lake of Fire. Imagine the armies of the earth gathering for one final battle, and the excitement they will feel as they all unite against God and His army. With this much might, they surely must believe God will be defeated. How that will all change when the beast and the false prophet are captured! All this was designed to prepare for God's rule. God's kingdom will be ready to begin its rule. Are you excited to live in a world that God is ruling as King, one in which all laws will honor Him? Will you be one who enters it?

### SAY WHAT?
Observation: What do I see?

### SO WHAT?
Interpretation: What does it mean?

### NOW WHAT?
Application: How does it apply to me?

### THEN WHAT?
Implementation: What do I do?

**XTRA READING**
REVELATION 19

## REVELATION 20:1-10

### SAY WHAT?

When did you, by faith, trust Christ as your Savior?

### SO WHAT?

What evidence do you see in your life that you have been truly saved?

### NOW WHAT?

How can you tell that your actions are the result of your salvation and not just outward conformity to Christianity?

### THEN WHAT?

In light of this passage, what personal commitment can you make?

Who are the rest of the dead referred to in verse 5? Where do the people who side with Satan at the end of the 1,000 years come from? To answer these questions, we must keep in mind some important facts. There are two resurrections mentioned in Scripture. The first one is of those who were saved when they died. That will take place at the Rapture. Those who have died without Christ will not be resurrected at this time. John was referring to these unsaved people in verse 5. Only those who are saved will enter into the 1,000 year reign of Christ. However, Christians who are alive on the earth at the end of the Tribulation will enter into the 1,000 year reign with their human bodies. These people will continue to have children throughout the 1,000 years. Although everyone will have to be obedient to Christ and His rule during this time, there will be some who will not turn to Christ for salvation. This proves that living in a perfect world, and doing all the right things outwardly, are not enough to make you a child of God. Man's heart changes only when he turns to Christ for salvation. No amount of outward effort or conformity will do. Have you allowed God to change your heart?

### XTRA READING
REVELATION 20

## NEW JERUSALEM

These last two chapters of Revelation address what it will be like in eternity for those of us who have accepted Christ as our Savior. Chapter 21 deals with the city of Jerusalem, and chapter 22 shows the blessing for us who will be living on the new earth forever. It is amazing, as you read through it, to discover all the wonderful things God has prepared for us. What makes this city even greater is not the material that is used to build it, nor the construction--not even its size. What makes it great is Who will be there. It is a city in which God will dwell. There will be no need for light, because His glory will shine. There will be no need for a temple, because He will be present for us to worship Him. Think about what it will be like to live there with your saved loved ones and friends, all the saints of the Bible, and especially Jesus Christ. It is going to be awesome! It is sobering, however, to realize there are those who will not be going to live in glory. If this is you, allow both the horrors of God's judgment and the glory of our eternal home, to motivate you to trust Christ. If it is someone you know and care for, be motivated to share Christ with them. Either way, act today.

### SAY WHAT?
Observation: What do I see?

### SO WHAT?
Interpretation: What does it mean?

### NOW WHAT?
Application: How does it apply to me?

### THEN WHAT?
Implementation: What do I do?

**XTRA READING**

REVELATION 21

## SAY WHAT?

Observation: What do I see?

## SO WHAT?

Interpretation: What does it mean?

## NOW WHAT?

Application: How does it apply to me?

## THEN WHAT?

Implementation: What do I do?

Well, your journey through the book of Revelation is over. You have just completed reading this amazing book. Hopefully, you leave it with a greater understanding of not only the end times, but of God as well. In the very first chapter, we read that blessings await those who read, hear, and take to heart the words of this book. As we have read of both the horrible things ahead for the unsaved, and the wonderful things ahead for God's people, we have rejoiced knowing that we will not experience the horrible things that will take place. Hopefully, you have a greater motivation to serve God more faithfully. Hopefully, you have gained a greater burden to reach the lost in your world with the message of salvation so that they may avoid the Tribulation and an eternity without Christ. Our time is slipping away and Jesus Christ will soon return. Make sure that you, and the people in your life, are ready for that day. Take some time today to reflect on what God confronted you with as you read Revelation this month. Don't walk away from it unchanged! Take some time to jot down ways you are committed to change.

**XTRA READING**

REVELATION 22